UPWAVE

For Joyce Chiu

Chiu Ngar Mei
Xiexie

Upwave
City Dynamics and the Coming Capitalist Revival

JOHN MONTGOMERY
Urban Cultures Ltd, UK and Australia

ASHGATE

Published by
Ashgate Publishing Limited
Wey Court East
Union Road
Farnham
Surrey, GU9 7PT
England

Ashgate Publishing Company
Suite 420
101 Cherry Street
Burlington
VT 05401-4405
USA

www.ashgate.com

British Library Cataloguing in Publication Data
Montgomery, John.
 Upwave : city dynamics and the coming capitalist revival.
 1. Urban economics. 2. Business cycles. 3. Economic
 development.
 I. Title
 330.9'1732-dc22

Library of Congress Cataloging-in-Publication Data
Montgomery, John, Dr.
 Upwave : city dynamics and the coming capitalist revival / by John Montgomery.
  p. cm.
 Includes bibliographical references and index.
 ISBN 978-1-4094-2226-6 (hardcover) -- ISBN 978-1-4094-2227-3
(ebook) 1. Capitalism. 2. Economic history--21st century. 3. Wealth. 4. Economic
development. I. Title.
 HB501.M72143 2011
 330.12'2--dc22

2011003885

ISBN 9781409422266 (hbk)
ISBN 9781409422273 (ebk)

Printed and bound in Great Britain by the
MPG Books Group, UK.

Contents

List of Figures and Tables

Figures

Tables

Acknowledgements

My thanks to my friends Pam and Ted Brennan and Rob Philps for reading and commenting on chapters in this book, and also to Michael Bollen and Stephanie Johnston. Phoebe Montgomery encouraged me to write this book and helped with the chapter outline. I'd like to record my appreciation of my publisher, Valerie Rose, and her colleagues at Ashgate. Jeff Humphreys and his colleague Mark Janz generously helped out with some of the diagrams. My friend the artist David Reid offered encouragement and knowledge of Japanese art. David Lock, as he often does, offered some kindly and wise advice.

Chapter 1

Prologue

There is a tide in the affairs of men,
Which, taken at the flood, leads on to fortune;
Omitted, all the voyage of their life,
Is bound in shallows and in miseries.
On such a full sea are we now afloat,
And we must take the current when it serves…

Shakespeare, *Julius Caesar*, 215

I sat down to write this book at the beginning of January 2009, less than three months after the collapse of Lehman Brothers Merchant Bank and the banking panic that followed. It was already clear that most of the world's economies were heading for a recession. Indeed, that what should have been a mild recessionary 'correction' was, by dint of the credit crunch or 'Global Financial Crisis' (as it came to be known), much more serious.

Even so, I was of the view that the pattern or terms of trade across the world had been strong with healthy growth being recorded, year on year, since the late 1990s. China and India were growing at something approaching 10 per cent per annum in 2006, Australia was growing at nearly 5 per cent, and countries such as Brazil, Russia and the Baltic states were also growing well. In the United States, however, consumer spending and confidence were slow to recover from the 9/11 attacks and levels of government debt were increasing.

Governments and central banks around the world from about 2005 began to take economic growth for granted. Indeed the focus of their efforts switched to controlling general price inflation, considered to be too high at 3 per cent. Central banks, led by Alan Greenspan in the United States, began to increase nominal interest rates in 2005 and kept doing so in 2006 and 2007. During the period June 2004 to September 2005 there were no fewer than 11 interest rate rises. Rates effectively doubled. By June 2007, the 30-year mortgage rate in the US was close to 7 per cent. This was designed to stop inflation in its tracks, which it eventually did for a short while, but the cost was a recession that was already gathering in early 2008, that is six months before Lehman Brothers. We can see this in the chart showing UK GDP growth, 2008–2010 (Figure 1.1), where it is clear that the recession began in the second quarter of 2008.

But the increase in interest rates had a much more devastating and unintended consequence. Borrowers of sub-prime mortgages in the United States began to default on their repayments, in very many cases simply walking away from their houses. Greenspan and his colleague Ben Bernanke were warned of this, but chose

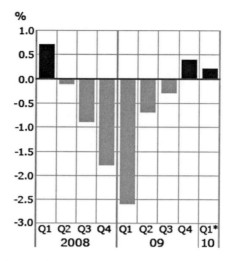

Figure 1.1 UK GDP growth, 2008–2010
Source: Beckman 1983.

to ignore these warnings. 'It's a blood bath', said Mark Kiesel, executive vice president of Newport Beach, California-based Pacific Investment Management Co., the manager of $668 billion in bond funds. 'We're talking about a two- to three-year downturn that will take a whole host of characters with it, from job creation to consumer confidence. Eventually it will take the stock market.'[1] 'It's not just a housing recession anymore, it looks more and more like an economic recession', said Nouriel Roubini, a Clinton administration Treasury Department director and economic adviser, head of Roubini Global Economics in New York.

By this time US investment banks, insurance companies, pension funds and asset-management firms held some $6 trillion of mortgage-backed securities. Subprime mortgages, given to people with bad or limited credit histories, accounted for about $800 billion of the market.

Over a short period of a few months in 2008, it became clear that these bad debts had been sold on through the banking system and that no one knew for sure how much debt was bad and who owned the paper. The 'contagion' swept from country to country as banks in Iceland, Ireland, the UK and Germany began to fail.

With the rising number of threatened bank failures, sources of lending dried up and we had what was then called the 'Credit Crunch'. Before long, falling confidence and panic caused businesses large and small to pull in their horns, sit tight and wait for the recovery – if there was one. Investors stopped investing and people stopped spending, businesses began to lay-off some of their employees.

---

1   Howley, Kathleen M., 'Rate Rise Pushes Housing, Economy to "Blood Bath"', *Bloomberg*, 20 June 2007.

What was supposed to be a mild downturn had become a full-blown global recession. During the autumn of 2008 the stock markets around the world lost roughly a third of their value. In the United States the housing market dropped by 18 per cent. Many pundits blamed this on greed and the over-valuation of stocks and shares, a stock market bubble if you like, without bothering to analyse how this state of affairs had come about.

The recession of 2008–2009 was caused initially by official interest rate policy, complicated somewhat by the banking collapse, a disaster waiting to happen. This was likewise triggered – but not caused – by increasing interest rates and hundreds of thousands of bad debtors in the US housing market. The root cause of this problem was bad lending to people who should never have been given loans. This was the outcome of government policy on 'affordable housing' for minorities and the activities of Fannie Mae and the oversight committees in the US Congress and Senate. Loans raised by Fannie Mae, to simplify, were bundled up as 'mortgage-backed securities' and sold onto the merchant banks – Goldman Sachs, Bear Stearns, Merrill Lynch, Lehmans – who, in turn, repackaged the bundles into 'consolidated securities' and sold these on to commercial or 'high street' banks.

At the end of the day, the big Wall Street banks were left with 30 per cent of all sub-prime losses. This explains why the deeds to a house sold in Arkansas could wind up being owned by a bank in Spain. That is, if anyone can ever work out which loan went where. This is rightly a cause for great anger and disbelief, but bear in mind that the banks were told that the loans bought up by Fannie Mae and repackaged were guaranteed by the US government. Interestingly, this analysis of the sub-prime crisis is shared by most independent economists,[2] who more or less agree that the roots of the crisis were cheap money, lax lending, mortgage-backed derivatives, consumer ignorance and the pushing of home ownership by the US government.

And this is the point. It is important we separate out the economic downturn or 'soft landing' that the central bankers were trying to orchestrate from the nasty surprise that became the 'Global Financial Crisis'. No one – or at least no central bankers – were expecting the 'GFC' because no one could believe people would be so stupid as to sell mortgages to people with very low incomes and then bundle up their loans as 'mortgage-backed securities' and sell them on through the banking system. No one thought anyone would be stupid enough to buy these 'products' either. But people did. And the result was an old-fashioned banking panic.[3]

It was clear that the banking collapse would only end once the bad debt had been burned out of the market and written-off, but the new Obama administration

---

2   See Lancaster, J., *Whoops! Why Everyone Owes Everyone and No One Can Pay* (New York: Allen Lane, 2010); Stiglitz, J., *Freefall: Free Markets and the Sinking of the Global Economy* (New York: Allen Lane, 2010); Lowenstein, R., *The End of Wall Street* (Melbourne: Scribe, 2010).

3   Montgomery, J., 'Social Engineers Make Bad Bankers', *The Australian*, 1 October 2008.

dithered over this for a period of six months. Now, however, the bad debt is gradually being removed from the banks, while foreclosed houses are being bought up by government agencies and third parties. The bad or 'toxic' debt is being washed from the system.

To be true, the banking panic rippled over and damaged the real or underlying economy and caused the economic downturn to morph into a serious recession. But is it really as bad as the Great Depression, when not-very-accurate data showed unemployment in the United States remained at levels over 20 per cent for seven years? Was 2009 a meltdown? It was certainly worrying and the outlook appeared bleak enough according to news reports and broadcasts. But something didn't make sense to me. Why was the US economy growing so strongly in June 2008, but devastated in October that very same year? Was the global economy really so fragile?

Political rhetoric at the time was also overblown. In the run-up to the US Presidential Election of November 2008, Barack Obama made repeated reference to the 'worst depression since the 1930s', blaming President Bush for 'having gotten us into this mess'. Other world leaders blamed the Americans, even although their own banks had bought bad debt. In the UK, the Prime Minister Gordon Brown blamed the UK's poor economic performance on the 'Global Financial Crisis', even nominating himself as the person to 'save the world'. Australia's Prime Minister Kevin Rudd warned that times were going to be 'very, very hard indeed'.

To an extent, these doom-laden warnings became a self-fulfilling prophecy as consumers and businesses stopped spending, partly because banks stopped lending. Governments and cental banks reacted by slashing interest rates and introducing large public spending programmes as 'stimulus' packages. And so the very same people who were warning of 'the inflation genie'[4] and were responsible for rapidly increasing interest rates in 2007 and early 2008,[5] were now cutting rates as low as they could go and spending very large amounts of public money. Both sets of measures cannot be right. If the economy was in free-fall in November 2008, why were interest rates increased as late as May of that year? If inflation was the major worry, why pump such large amounts of money into the economic system? Presumably, politicians and central bankers would tell us that they were reacting to events and the stimulus packages were necessary to avert a deep recession. Fair point, one might agree, but why if these people know so much did they increase rates so catastrophically the two years previously? The answer is that politicians and central bankers were caught napping by the Credit Crunch and, in some panic, over-reacted.[6]

---

4   Wayne Swan, Australian Treasurer, 1 February 2008.

5   As late as 16 July 2008, Ben Bernanke testified to a Congressional hearing that inflation was the biggest threat to the US economy. In June that same year, he argued that the threat of an economic downturn had 'diminished'.

6   'Reserve Bank Blundered: Costello', *The Australian*, 29 October 2008.

It is important also to understand that during the period 1929–1939 there was indeed a stock market collapse, a banking collapse and a very severe recession. But on that occasion the rate of profitability had been declining for some 10 years, so that the crash was an almighty correction in the first instance. This in turn triggered debt default, foreclosure, bankruptcy and a banking collapse, followed by firms going bust and people losing their jobs. By contrast, until mid 2008, the economy was growing and expanding nicely and the underlying conditions of demand and supply were strong. Inflation was low, and profitability was increasing; new technologies, new goods and services, were finding new markets, and countries such as China, India and Brazil were growing their internal domestic markets.

If the comparison with the 1930s is erroneous, is there any other period of modern economic history that is more relevant to today's situation? The example I would point to is the recession of 1953–1954, long since faded from memory. This followed the 'Wool Inflation' of 1951–1952, caused by increased demand for uniforms for the Korean War. Policy-makers were alarmed when inflation reached 6 per cent, and set about a policy of fiscal and monetary tightening. The result was a year-long recession, with inflation not surprisingly falling to zero. Growth returned during 1954, and by 1957 inflation was back at 4 per cent. Policy was again tightened, leading to another recession in 1957–1958. This was known in the United States as the 'Eisenhower Recession', where GDP fell in the last quarter of 1957 by nearly 3 per cent – with the radical Left predicting the collapse of capitalism. It was around this time that Harold Macmillan in the UK was insisting we 'have never had it so good'. There ensued a 15-year period of strong economic growth, culminating in the peak of profitability in 1973. The 1960s were a golden age. Perhaps, I beg to suggest, it is time for another one.

In the absence of a much-trailed 'double dip', there should be no 1930s-style 10-year depression. The recession should be relatively short-lived. Healthy demand should return with confidence. Indeed, as of March 2010, as I write this, the OECD[7] is forecasting growth of 10 per cent for China, 7 per cent for India and 5 per cent for Brazil and Russia during 2010. In Singapore, growth for 2010 reached 13–15 per cent, although this is projected to flatten out to 6 per cent in 2011.[8] Things, it seems, are already on the up. But there is a sting in the tail. Two, actually.

Unfortunately, many Western governments have been over-spending, before, during and after the 'Global Financial Crisis', such that the greatest risk to economies in the second half of 2010 is now 'sovereign risk' (governments defaulting on their bonds) and falling credit ratings for countries such as Greece, Portugal, Spain and Ireland. This may come to be seen as a new 'Fiscal Crisis of the State' where governments struggle to contain spending and debt.[9] In Europe, Germany stands

---

7 The Organization for Economic Cooperation and Development, based in Paris.

8 *The Straits Times*, 28 November 2010.

9 A book by this title was published by James O'Conner in 1973. O'Conner writes from a Marxist perspective – legitimacy and hegemony of the capitalist state – and so his analysis is unhelpful.

out in its attempts to regain lost productivity and hold wages and export prices down. Even France is trying to bring government spending under control. But in Britain public spending and government debt reached record levels: in 2010 it is running a budget deficit amounting to 12.8 per cent of GDP, not far behind Greece which, in April 2010, had to call for help from the International Monetary Fund to reduce its growing levels of debt. In Belgium, the sovereign debt is 100 per cent of GDP. The UK's total government debt as of April 2010 now stands at 60 per cent of GDP. Swingeing cuts in public services have been prescribed in order to balance the national accounts, yet these only take Britain back to 2002 levels of spending.[10] This situation is in danger of undermining the Euro currency and the notion of the European Union itself – which boils down to the cross-subsidisation of poor countries and regions by the economically dynamic.

The second problem is that the US recovery is fragile. The bulk of new jobs created in 2009 and the first half of 2010 were in government; relatively few jobs were created by the private sector which, instead, has continued to lay people off. In June 2010, the US economy shed 125,000 FTE jobs. Partly as a result, US consumer prices in June 2010 were actually falling. Unemployment remains at close to 10 per cent. Although many US firms are now trading profitably, they are running up profits rather than seeking to expand and take on new staff. Why should this be? The answer is that business confidence in the Obama administration is low: people are expecting government debt to continue rising, for returns on investment to fall and for new taxes on businesses and the wealthy to be introduced. Moreover, many industries – notably the automobile industry – are now effectively owned by the government, so no one will invest there. And, as was the case under the New Deal, government is attempting to set wage rates across the country for various industrial sectors. The result is that private investors are loath to risk their money. The only way to end the US recession properly will be to unleash a wave of investment in expansion, new innovations, products and services, and markets – including export markets; and a return of consumer spending. If this begins to happen, economic growth should strengthen during the second half of 2010, although it will probably remain at modest levels of 2–3 per cent per annum until 2012.

The basic argument of this book is that economies grow in waves: there is a tide in the growth and decline of economies, and with them, great cities and civilisations and art. This will be explained in more detail in Chapter 2, but the general argument as posited by Joseph Schumpeter[11] is that a process of invention, innovation, new technological developments and thus new products, services and processes, kicks in every 50 years or so, bringing in a 'wave' of rapid wealth

---

10   A new Coalition Government, elected in May 2010, has the task of reducing public debt and deficit, cutting public spending, and restoring market confidence in government bonds.

11   Schumpeter, J., *Business Cycles* (New York: McGraw-Hill, 1939; Philadelphia: Porcupine Press, reprinted 1982).

creation. Economies experience ups and downs along this longer curve, with mild downturns every nine years or so and booms in infrastructure investment roughly every 25 years. If the wave theory is correct, then in broad terms we are presently about 10 years into an upwave or period of growth, based on new industries, technologies and markets.

The field of macroeconomics has evolved in an attempt to smooth out the peaks and troughs of capitalist economic development, most famously posited by John Maynard Keynes[12] as 'demand management', and later by Monetarists as balancing inflation against unemployment.[13] But the effect more often than not is simply to make matters worse by over-correction, as I shall explain in Chapter 3. The peaks of inflation are higher and the troughs of low growth are deeper. This is similar – to use a metaphor – to 'control oscillation' in aviation, such that by over-correction a pilot succeeds merely in putting the aircraft into a spin. This occurs both under Monetarism (the control of interest rates) and Keynesianism (government spending). If true, then it is largely pointless for governments and central banks to intervene at the macro-level, other than maintaining control over the money supply. Governments would be wise to concentrate on providing a sound and stable – in the sense of not being prone to sudden changes of policy – business environment through such measures as reducing red tape, simplifying regulation and keeping business taxes low.

Economies, as I explain in Chapter 4, are much more complex and complicated than simplistic Monetary Theory – or Keynesianism or neo-classical econometrics – suggests. Some economists now argue that economics is really a form of ecosystem and that such systems incorporate their own checks and balances and feedback loops, in the form of price signals, balance of trade figures and currency valuations. Economies are dynamic, fluid, open systems that make themselves up as they go along. Moreover, economies are based in real places at the level of the city and region, not at the statistically convenient but largely unimportant level of the nation state. London is a city region of great complexity and dynamism; Edinburgh and Belfast are not. Successful national economies are in fact an amalgam of various propulsive places – cities, regions, small nation states – often coupled to laggard regions such as the Mezzogiorno, Wales or South Australia. Examples of such places are discussed in Chapter 5.

But why do some places prosper and others stagnate or even decline? Nearness to markets and raw materials is a traditional answer to this, although perhaps not as important as in earlier times. True, there are still resource regions and agricultural regions, but these days economic life revolves around cities and their immediate regions as sites of innovation and new work, grafting on to earlier rounds of wealth

---

12   Keynes, J. M., *The General Theory of Employment, Interest and Money* (London: Macmillan, 1936).

13   Friedman, M., *Capitalism and Freedom* (Chicago: University of Chicago Press, 1962).

creation and industries. Much of this, in the modern economy, revolves around industries of knowledge and meaning.

It is important to realise that wealth creation cannot be taken for granted. Politics and ideology can undermine economic development, as I explain in Chapter 7, and this usually boils down to taxation levels, government spending on welfare programmes, and the extent to which investment, risk-taking and entrepreneurship is encouraged or disparaged. It is important to consider the question of how far state intervention in economies should proceed before an economy is no longer a market economy but a command or centrally planned economy. The 'tipping point' looms into view where governments extract more than 35 per cent in taxes.

The arguments put forward in this book are as follows. Economies grow in waves or business cycles, enjoying periodic episodes of great prosperity, during the course of which leading cities enjoy golden ages of wealth creation and artistic development. Such a wave is currently underway, the 2008–2009 recession notwithstanding. The recent recession was caused by the sub-prime panic and the collapse of confidence in the banks, and was triggered by official interest rate policy during the period 2005–2008. Economies should recover rapidly as the terms of trade recover. This is because the markets for new and established goods and services are growing. Trade is the key to prosperity. Trade, moreover, occurs between cities and city regions rather than nation states as economic entities, and growth is thus dependent on the existence of dynamic city and city-region economies. Orthodox economic theory and policy fails to understand this simple truth. The Western economic system – or capitalism – is in the growth phase of an upwave, as I argue in Chapter 6, and so the next 20 years or so will be a time of plenty, a golden age.

The point is to understand that capitalism is a good thing, it brings benefits in wealth, the quality of life, raises life expectancy, and it provides taxes to fund social programmes and environmental husbandry. It lifts people out of grinding poverty. Since 1935, real GDP across the world (after inflation) has increased ten-fold; in Europe average real GDP per capita multiplied by a factor of four. During the past 200 years, since the beginning of modern capitalism – the Great Depression notwithstanding – average wealth in Western capitalist economies has doubled every generation. The rate of wealth creation varies from country to country depending on the business environment found in each; and the rate of growth depends too on where we are in the business cycle at any given point in time. Capitalism thrives under conditions of individual liberty and choice, minimal state intervention in markets, social stability and the rule of law. Where these conditions exist, growth will follow, and every 50 years or so we shall find ourselves living in a golden age.

Chapter 2
The Long Waves of Capitalist Growth

The fundamental impulse that sets and keeps the capitalist engine in motion comes from the new consumers' goods, the new methods of production or transportation, the new forms of industrial organization that capitalist enterprise creates ... (This) process of industrial mutation ... incessantly revolutionizes the economic structure from within, incessantly destroying the old one, incessantly creating a new one. This process of Creative Destruction is the essential fact about capitalism.

Joseph Schumpeter, *Capitalism, Socialism and Democracy*, 1943

Business Cycles

For the past 500 years, but most rapidly since the 1780s, Western economies have developed in periodic spurts of wealth creation, artistic development and physically as we build new cities. This process is as old as capitalism itself. Long periods of economic growth are followed by periods of stagnation and low growth, as night follows day. This occurs because the goods and services associated with particular phases of growth become exhausted, in the sense that there are no longer profitable markets to be sold into. The outcome is that particular goods and services – cotton in the eighteenth century, steel and transport in the nineteenth, automobiles and electric goods in the early twentieth, consumer electronics in the late twentieth – reach the limits to market penetration. Because of this the level of sales fall, prices are cut, the rate of profit falls, share prices fall, businesses fail, jobs are lost and a cycle of decline sets in as aggregate levels of demand fall again.[1]

The only way out of such downturns or slumps is for a set of new products to be brought to the market, a range of goods and services for which no market previously existed. For this to happen, such goods and services need to be invented. This almost always involves the application of new technologies to either invent whole new products, or else to production processes to increase productivity or improve design. For, as advances in technologies are applied commercially, sales will increase, profit levels will rise, economic growth will follow and so too will wealth creation. The next wave of growth is then underway.

In this way, the capitalist or market economy follows a pattern of growth and contraction, similar to business cycles but over a much longer period. For each of these long waves of wealth creation, the crucial development – sometimes more so than the original invention – is its application by one or more creative entrepreneurs.

---

1 This chapter is a reworking of material originally published in my book *The New Wealth of Cities* (Aldershot: Ashgate, 2007).

Markets for new products develop and produce a period of economic growth, an upwave, during which time the rate of profit rises with volumes of trade and the general level of wealth increases. The result is a profit cycle over a long period of some 54 years that operates alongside shorter cycles over periods of nine and 27 years. Broadly speaking it works as illustrated in Table 2.1.

Table 2.1 The business cycle

TOP OF THE BOOM

Going Up

Rising interest rates	Falling demand
Rising real estate prices	Falling rates of profit
Rising share prices	Falling share prices
Increasing demand	Falling interest rates
New products and services	Rising real estate prices
New inventions	

Coming Down

DEPTH OF DEPRESSION

The argument put forward in this book is that we are in the growth phase of a long business cycle, brought about by new technology, new products and services and expanded markets.

The Long Waves

According to the Soviet economist Nicolai Kondratieff, economic growth and wealth creation under capitalism follows a pattern of 30-year growth cycles interspersed with 25-year slumps. Kondratieff argued that this was because the economic 'exploitation' of existing technologies had been exhausted, so that growth could only come from a new generation of technologies.[2] Each cycle lasts for roughly 55–60 years, with peaks of economic growth at the mid-point:

> The upswing in the first long wave embraces the period from 1789 to 1814, i.e. 25 years; its decline begins in 1814 and ends in 1849, a period of 35 years. The cycle is therefore completed in 60 years. The rise in the second wave begins in 1847 and ends in 1873, lasting 24 years. The decline of the second wave begins

2   Kondratieff, N. D., *The Long Wave Cycle* (New York: Richardson and Snyder, 1984).

in 1873 and ends in 1896, a period of 23 years. The length of the second wave is 47 years. The upward movement of the third wave begins in 1896 and ends in 1920, its duration 24 years. The decline of the wave, according to the data, begins in 1920.[3]

Karl Marx[4] had earlier argued that capitalism is subject to periodic crises or changes caused, he argued, by 'under-consumption' or falling demand. Marx saw capitalism as inherently contradictory because of 'class conflict' over 'surplus value'. He foretold of a 'pauperisation' of the working class, violent revolution and a collapse of capitalism to be replaced by Communism. Most of his economic theory is unhelpful. The observation that capitalist economies have booms and busts does not depend on historical materialism's fixation with class analysis. It is however possible that, as a Soviet economist, Kondratieff used Marx's ideas of crises as a starting point.

Later, John Maynard Keynes would argue that governments should intervene to correct economic instability. Keynes, in seeking to understand why there should be a Great Depression, and what could be done to lower unemployment, came to the conclusion, like Marx, that the problem lay in falling demand.

Using commodity prices, Kondratieff was able to show that periods of strong growth occur every 45–55 years, separated by periods of sharp decline. Between 1814 and 1843, for example, prices fell by 59 per cent. From 1843, economies were growing once more – prices jumped 33 per cent between 1852 and 1854 alone. Prices levelled off and began to fall again from 1864, leading to a deep recession which only bottomed out in 1894. By the late 1890s prices were increasing again, albeit slowly. By 1920, business was booming but prices peaked that very year. This was disguised for a while during the Roaring Twenties, but led finally to the 'Great Crash' of 1929.

Since the late 1780s, there have been four long waves.[5] The first of these began in England and France in the 1780s, following a period of deep depression made all the worse by the South Sea Bubble in England and the Mississippi Bubble in France. The depression was characterised by a collapse in raw material prices, especially wheat, and bottomed out in around 1783. By 1789, prices were beginning to rise again, surging from 1798, during which time Britain and France were at war. A further surge occurred in 1812 but within two years prices and economic activity had passed their peak. A sharp downturn occurred in 1815, followed by a short-lived period of 'secondary prosperity', known at the time as the 'Era of Good Feelings'. By 1819, the economy was once again in recession, triggered by a collapse in wheat prices, and followed by a similar collapse in cotton a few years later. Land prices in the United States fell, and the long depression would last from

3   Ibid.

4   Marx, K., *Capital: A Critique of Political Economy: Volume 3, Part 1, The Process of Capitalist Production as a Whole, 1867* (New York: Cosimo Books, 1996).

5   Beckman, R., *The Downwave* (London: Pan Books, 1983).

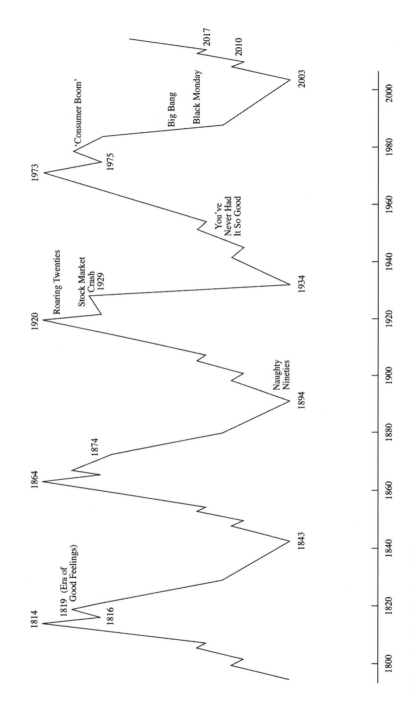

Figure 2.1 The Kondratieff waves

the 1820s to the 1840s. Between 1814 and 1843, prices fell by 59 per cent. The first wave had lasted 54 years.

The second wave kicked in from 1843, led by industrial production, and an upturn in exports and commodity prices. Between 1852 and 1854, consumer prices leapt by 33 per cent. The peak came in 1864. In 1873, a series of financial panics in Germany signalled the onset of a deep depression. This would last until 1896, so that the second wave lasted 54 years. Prices began to recover in the late 1890s, and began to increase steadily until 1920 when the commodity market collapsed. This time the speculative bubble that burst was in Argentina. The recession lasted for two years and was followed by a period of secondary prosperity – the 'Roaring Twenties' during which time fortunes were made on the stock market, fashions changed dramatically and liquor consumption increased. The crash came in 1929, followed by a severe depression which hit its lowest level in 1934. The recovery was led to a significant extent by rearming for war, but also from the emergence of new technologies and, later, consumer products. The third wave also lasted some 54 years.

The fourth wave was clearly underway by the mid 1950s. Britain was booming, as indeed were the United States, Germany and later Japan. This time around the growth industries were civil aviation, plastics, pharmaceuticals, household goods and consumer electronics. The upwave lasted throughout the 1960s and early 1970s, peaking in 1974. The short recession of 1973–1975 was followed by the 'consumer boom' of the mid 1970s, driven by rising house prices and the expansion of credit. The main secondary depression kicked in from the early 1980s, and was evidenced at the time by falling commodity and factory gate prices, falling oil prices and falling property prices. This much was evident when Beckman wrote *The Downwave*[6] (published in 1983). Beckman went on to forecast the stock market collapse of 1987, the property boom of the late 1980s and the long recession throughout the 1990s. This was characterised by very low growth in the 1990s as the depression bottomed out, a stagnant stock market and a switch of investment once more into property. The stock market only began to make real gains in 2004, by which time the upwave was already in train. The fourth wave lasted from around 1949 to 2003, again a period of 54 years.

Peaks and Troughs

A pattern across the waves can be seen. Peaks in commodity prices occur every 54 years – in 1920 and 1974, and in 1868 and 1814. These peaks are followed by a 'corrective' recession which lasts for two years or so, in turn followed by a short recovery. There then follows a stock market collapse, as in 1929 and 1987, a fall in interest rates, a property boom and a deep depression. That is, until the next upwave begins.

---

6   Ibid.

This then certainly appears to explain the existence of periodic booms in economic development and wealth creation, as brought about by new technologies, production processes and consumer goods and services. In this way the economic cycle follows four broad phases: an upwave, followed by a recession, followed by a period of secondary prosperity, followed by a secondary recession.

IDEALISED ECONOMIC LONG WAVE MODEL

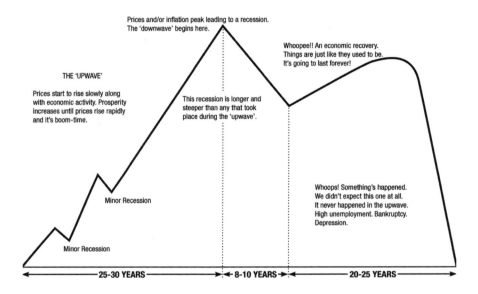

Figure 2.2 The long wave: idealised model

Each wave differs from the others in the detail of technologies, industries, levels of wealth already existing, consumers, geography, leading cities, leading nations and so on. But the waves all share certain characteristics or phases of development.

The upwave gets underway and peaks after 25–30 years. Prices start to rise slowly along with economic activity; prosperity increases. There is then a minor recession, after about seven years, and lasting for a year or so. The upwave then continues but prices increase again and a correction leads to another mild recession after about eight years. There then follows some 15 years of prosperity and boom-times. The peak of the upwave occurs at about the 25–30 year mark, for example in 1973 or 1920. The recession that follows lasts about 8–10 years, longer and deeper than the previous two, the most recent example being 1973–1982. The economy then experiences a secondary economic boom and times are good, for example in 1982–1987 or 1920–1929. Everyone is then caught by surprise as the

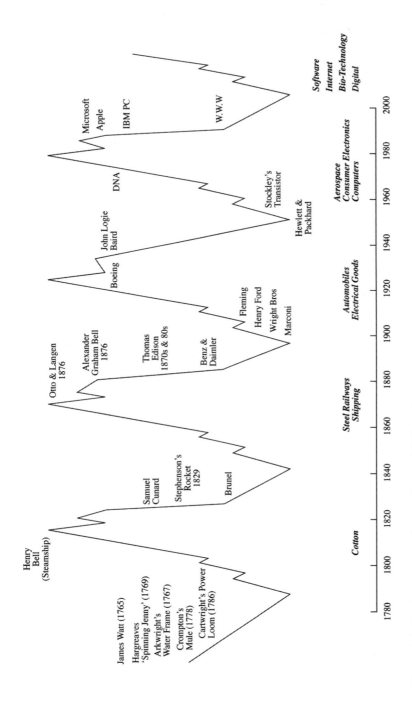

Figure 2.3 The long waves: innovation and industries

stock market collapses, as it did in 1929, 1987 and in the Great Panic of 1873. The deepest recession of the cycle follows, and this lasts for about 12 years of downturn, recession, recovery and low growth, for example the period 1991 to 2002. By this time the economy is embarking upon its next long wave.

Kondratieff would not live to see the end of the third wave, the crash and Great Depression of the 1930s: he died in a Siberian concentration camp, found guilty of being a heretic and harbouring dangerous views on economic development. The Kondratieff waves have been the subject of much debate amongst economists and academics for over 60 years now. Robert Beckman plots a fourth wave which he dates from 1946 to 2000. Writing in 1983, he predicted the onset of a 'secondary depression' from 1983/1984, leading to a stock market collapse and followed by a deep trough which would bottom out in the early to mid 1990s.

New Technologies and New Industries

The most serious work on long wave business cycles was carried out by Joseph Schumpeter at Harvard University in the 1930s.[7] Schumpeter confirmed three 'Kondratieff cycles', each associated with the rise of new industries: from 1789 (the early industrial revolution), from the 1840s (the age of steam, steel, rail and ships) and from 1896 (electricity, motor cars and 'Fordism'). Schumpeter stressed that the important point is not the invention of a technology, but rather its applications to commerce, trade and production processes. He argued that economic growth is triggered by the emergence of new groups of entrepreneurs, prepared to take on new forms of work just as previous generations are tiring, dying or retiring! He saw this as a sort of 'generational struggle' between old money and new wealth creators or 'new men'. Schumpeter saw that economies, of necessity, grow in spurts because entrepreneurial behaviour lies at the heart of all economic activity. This, in turn, generates new applications for and combinations of technologies, using human skills to generate new industries and products. For Schumpeter, this is a process of 'creative destruction' where the new evolves from, replaces and supplants the old.

Moreover, Schumpeter argued, the new innovations would tend to be invented during periods of economic depression, would then generate new processes and products and the next upswing would happen. This seems obvious enough in hindsight, when we look back at the inventions of Richard Arkwright, Thomas Edison, Otto Benz, Alexander Fleming, Bill Gates, Henry Bell or the Wright Brothers. But at the time, their inventions were revolutionary.

Writing in 1939, Schumpeter would know that the next upswing – lasting roughly until 1974 – was about to happen. As it turned out, the technologies this time around were electronics, commercial aviation, consumer household

---

7   Schumpeter, J., *Business Cycles* (New York: McGraw-Hill, 1939; Philadelphia: Porcupine Press, reprinted 1982).

goods, radio and sound-recording. These technologies would become exhausted, to varying degrees, by the 1970s and 1980s, at which point new technologies were being invented and/or applied. Thus the period 1975–2000 roughly equates with a Kondratieff depression, during which time the general rate of profit fell, older industries declined, unemployment rose and new technologies – in this case computers, digital media and pharmaceuticals – were invented and began to be applied commercially. If this is true, then it seems likely that the capitalist economy in the year 2000 entered an upswing that will last for 25 to 30 years, that is until 2030 or thereabouts.

Schumpeter himself drew upon the work of two other economists, Kitchin and Juglar, both of whom argued that market economies develop along the path of a business cycle. Juglar's cycle lasts nine years, and is based on the fluctuation in commodity prices. Economic growth and prosperity brings higher prices, exports become more difficult and foreign exchange moves out of the country. The end of the cycle is marked by the ending of price rises. Schumpeter discovered that Juglar's 1919 peak coincided with the longer Kondratieff wave peak at the end of a long period of prosperity; but at the following Juglar peak in 1928, the long wave was already in a downswing and this combination led to the collapse in stock markets and the global economy.

Juglar divided his cycle into three periods: prosperity, crisis and liquidation, which appear also to correspond with Kitchin's 40-month business cycle – that is to say growth and decline occurs within all three of Juglar's periods. Simon Kuznets[8] would later argue that the long waves last only for 22–25 years and are in fact based on variations in construction activity. The geographer Brian Berry,[9] writing in 1970, proposed that both economists were correct. In fact, argued Barry, the Kuznets waves operate within the longer Kondratieff cycle, so that each Kondratieff wave has two Kuznets booms in construction. Within these 20–25 year cycles, the shorter Juglar cycles sit at a ratio of three Juglars to a Kuznets, and therefore six Juglars to a Kondratieff. This led Beckman, writing in 1983, to conclude that the periods of 'acute panic and danger' in the world economy occur where all three cycles are in downswing simultaneously. This occurred in 1974 and again in 1983. It also occurred in 1992 and 2001, by which time the global economy was approaching the start of a Kondratieff upswing. The next Juglar downswing was at its depth in 2009, but by that time the fifth Kondratieff wave was well underway.

Although long wave theory is no longer taught in university courses on economics and economic geography – preferring no doubt the rigours of gender studies and post-modernism – it is reappearing in the work of economic think

---

8 Kuznets, S., 'Schumpeter's Business Cycles', *American Economic Review*, 30, 1940, 250–71.

9 Berry, B. J. L., *Long-Wave Rhythms in Economic Development and Political Behavior* (Baltimore: Johns Hopkins University Press, 1991).

tanks. For example, Professor John Foster,[10] in February 2010, published a policy paper on productivity and innovation, as a contribution to the Australian government's drive to increase innovation in the Australian economy.[11] Following Schumpeter, Foster argues that the key to economic progress is entrepreneurship or what Margaret Thatcher termed 'wealth creators', after Hayek. How well individual countries do during upswings is dependent on culture, law, politics and the actions of governments, so that 'policy settings' and the approach to taxation and public spending can and do help or hinder wealth creation. The test is whether these settings support or impede entrepreneurship. Not surprisingly, we find a number of Western governments are now commissioning reports on innovation and entrepreneurship.[12]

A recent important contribution by Carlota Perez[13] argues, following Kondratieff and Schumpeter, that economic growth takes place in successive surges of about half a century, and these are driven by a technological revolution. She posits that there are six 'predictable' stages to these surges: technological revolution, financial bubble, collapse, golden age of prosperity and political unrest. It is worth delving into Perez's work further.

According to Perez, each technological revolution leads to an investment frenzy as would-be entrepreneurs seek to get ahead of the game, and as they convince the financial sector to lend them money. This might seem irrational to some, but in truth each and every entrepreneur is acting very rationally indeed. She gives the example of the dot.com boom and bust of the late 1990s, but the railways in the mid nineteenth century followed a similar path. The ensuing over-development and over-valuing of new investments – Perez characterises this as a 'divorce between paper and real value' – is followed by a crash, but this crash is short-lived as the economy generally is on a growth trajectory. The bubble and collapse is thus followed by a golden age of wealth creation as markets develop, capacity is increased and demand is increased. The final stage, political unrest, sets in as real inflation reappears, productivity stagnates, full employment is reached and trades unions make unreasonable demands for wage increases. Precisely this happened in the late 1960s and early 1970s. As the economy moves into a long downswing, certain old industries begin to decline and unemployment increases.

If Perez is correct, as I believe she is, then the world economy is entering a phase of 'Synergy' or a long period of 'coherent economic growth based on

---

10   Foster, J., *Productivity, Creative Destruction and Innovation Policy* (Sydney: The Australian Business Foundation, February 2010).

11   See for example the *Venturous Australia Report*, 2008.

12   See the Sainsbury Report: *The Race to the Top: A Review of Government's Science and Innovation Policies* (London: HMSO, 2007). Also *Rising Above the Gathering Storm: Energising and Employing America for a Brighter Economic Future* (Washington, DC: National Academies Press, 2008).

13   Perez, C., *Technological Revolutions and Financial Capital: The Dynamics of Bubbles and Golden Ages* (Cheltenham: Edward Elgar, 2002).

increasing production and employment and a "recoupling" of real and paper wealth'. This, then, is a golden age. As it matures, the recently new industries – plasma televisions, mobile phones – reach technological limits and market saturation, at which point industrial and financial capital decouple once more, the latter switching into property.

John Foster argues that the important role for governments is to balance new rules and regulations that provide greater security with those that keep the economic system open enough to allow new growth. He sees this as an offshoot of evolutionary or complex economics (which we shall discuss more fully in Chapter 3). Foster argues that there are

> no less than six coinciding elements (that determine) the strength of a long upswing: organisational innovation, technological innovation, institutional innovation, available finance, available skills and available physical energy.[14]

Countries who offer a strong combination of these conditions, argues Foster, will succeed, those who do not will fare badly in the global recovery. It will be noted that these are all essentially 'supply side' measures, to which we might add a simple tax system, less red tape, low taxes and a limit on government spending.

Modes of Production

Four different eras of capitalist economic development coincide with the Kondratieff long waves of the capitalist business cycle. During these various eras of capitalist economic development, the way in which production itself was organised also varied.

Thus early capitalism was based on craft production organised by guilds and the merchant class; early industrial capitalism produced the 'Dark Satanic Mills' and a more rapid urbanisation; industrial capitalism was based on factory production and was organised by industrial producers – so-called Fordism; and late capitalism was and is characterised by flexible specialisation, the putting-out mode of production and is largely organised by service producers. It also would appear that different forms of production can survive and be carried over into a later age when the dominant mode of production is changing. Thus the bespoke tailoring of Savile Row and the jewellery industry of Hatton Gardens, both in London, still operate as craft guilds, more or less. Likewise, the film industry of the 1920s to the 1950s was essentially a form of factory production organised by the studio system. Whereas Hollywood today is a hybrid of the studio system combined with a classic post-Fordist network of independent producers and sub-contracted specialists.

---

14 Foster, J. *Productivity, Creative Destruction and Innovation Policy* (Sydney: The Australian Business Foundation, February 2010), p. 17.

Industries such as the car industry in Japan or Korea are post-Fordist to the extent that production models are differentiated, but remain largely Fordist in that production occurs along assembly lines. Modern computers were invented in the 1940s and 1950s, and would later revolutionise electronics and consumer household goods; yet their biggest impact is only now being witnessed in the age of digitisation and the convergence of computer technology and all manner of service industries.

Table 2.2 Long-wave modes of production showing typical goods and services

Long Wave Cycle	Mode of Production	Organised by	Typical Goods and Services
1. 1781–1840	Late mercantile	Merchants and craft guilds	Clothing
2. 1840–1890	Early mass production	Industrialists	Rail, heavy engineering
3. 1890–1946	Mass production	Industrialists	Cars, electrical goods
4. 1946–2004	Flexible specialisation	Service providers	Computers, electronics, aviation, consumer, household goods
5. 2004–2060	Personalised consumption	Arbiters of taste	Design objects and art

Source: Montgomery, 2007.

The technologies that gave rise to the cotton industry were invented by Kay, Hargreaves and Arkwright in the mid-eighteenth century: the boom which followed would last until 1810 or thereabouts. The technologies of steel pressing, steam engines, railways and steam ships were invented in the early nineteenth century, prompting a boom that would last until the 1880s. Important inventions by Otto and Langen, Benz and Daimler, Edison, Alexander Graham Bell and Marconi would develop as the new industries of the twentieth century. Innovations by Turing, Hewlett and Packard, Jack Kilby at Texas Instruments and Stockley would lead to the computer age, micro-chips and consumer electronics. New innovations in software in the 1970s would enable the development of personal computers, laptops and various communications devices, as well as the Internet. It is notable that most of the primary inventions occur at the end of a downwave, that is to say as scientific and technological devices of the previous paradigm are over-exploited.

The origins of the next Kondratieff wave (2002 to around 2060) are already in place. That these industries will emerge from IT, communications, digitisation and forms of cultural creativity is in little doubt. They will also include bio-technology and environmental technologies. Many of these will continue to be organised on a post-Fordist model for several years at least; others will need to change more rapidly, that is, where the relationship between the producer and the consumer is closest. The creative industries are one of the key growth sectors of the fifth wave. As in previous waves, the impact of the knowledge and creative economies will be most keenly felt in the cities.

Thus, it may well be that the emerging mode of production will be towards what we shall term 'individualised consumption' and 'peer group purchasing' (communities of interest who collect certain art or objects, or who have hobbies and enthusiasms in common). Importantly, changes in style, fashion and taste will be mediated by what we might term 'arbiters of taste', that is to say fashion, art and music critics writing in 'lifestyle' magazines.

Again, if true, this means that more artists and designers will make a living from direct commissions, exhibitions and gallery openings. The independent gallery/shop will be a more important point-of-sale in future. Artists and designers will increasingly be entrepreneurs too, and as such will need entrepreneurial skills. They will create new work and sell it locally, nationally and globally. For the Internet and digital technologies (and air travel) will allow them to operate in markets beyond the places in which they themselves live. Many such businesses will be exporting firms, many will inter-trade locally and more will collaborate with other cultural entrepreneurs elsewhere. What is being described here is a new relationship between artistic and traditional craft skills, new design, new technology (of design and marketing as well as production) and new entrepreneurialism. The currency of such activities is ideas, skills and creativity.

Property Booms

Peter Hall[15] has argued, that because of the Kuznets curve (the 25-year construction peak as proposed by Simon Kuznets, discussed earlier), each Kondratieff cycle has two booms in construction activity, one coming with the upswing and the other 'just before the descent into depression: the 1900s and 1920s are obvious examples'. These would correspond with the mid 1950s and the early 1970s during the fourth Kondratieff wave.

Hall argues that the property boom during an upswing is due to investment in new plant, property and transport infrastructure; while the second property boom is characterised by speculation in land and property as the rate of profit in the economy falls – investors switch from stocks and shares into land and property. This certainly would seem to explain what happened in the 1950s and early 1970s, but what of the booms of the 1930s, or more recently the late 1980s and *fin de siècle*?

My own view is that, just as there are three Juglar cycles to a Kuznets (and therefore six to a Kondratieff), there are two property cycles to a Kuznets, and therefore four to a Kondratieff. This would mean, roughly speaking, there would be a property boom peak every 13 to 15 years. If true, we would expect to find

15   Hall, P., *Cities in Civilization* (London: Weidenfeld and Nicolson, 1998), p. 16.

property booms peaking in 1959, 1973, 1987 and 2002. Of these, we know that there were strong booms followed by property crashes in 1973 and 1987, the first owing to the end of the upswing and the second at a point where speculation in land and property became fevered following a stock market collapse. The major growth boom occurred during the 1950s (with transport infrastructure opening up new viable locations, and also rebuilding after the war), and its continuation into the 1960s was most likely simply a reflection of growing general prosperity. The boom of the late 1990s would appear to be a reaction to low returns in the stock market.

Thus, we can posit that there are four important property booms to every Kondratieff wave, as follows. First, the boom of the first quarter of the Kondratieff wave driven by new investment in transport technologies and construction, with the largest increases in value during the second seven years of the upswing – the 1900s and the late 1950s. This period of property development is an outcome of general economic growth. Second, the boom of the early part of the second quarter occurs where increases in general prosperity feed through into home ownership – the early 1920s and the 1960s. This period marks the spread of wealth into new home ownership, and is often associated with over-development and urban sprawl.

The boom of the end of the third quarter, that is the crisis point at which the rate of profit becomes negative and investment switches into speculative property trading – the late 1920s and the late 1980s. This is a speculative boom which inevitably crashes. Finally, the boom of the end of the downswing occurs when the rate of return on other investments is historically low – the late 1930s (interrupted by the war), the late 1990s and early 2000s. This boom makes up some of the losses of the preceding crash and reflects the fact that the downswing is beginning to bottom out. The boom at the beginning of the upwave may not be especially noticeable, at first, compared to the others, but is an important indication that the upswing is underway. I would expect this to become evident after 2010 as the growth period of the fifth Kondratieff wave takes hold.

Leading Cities

Wealth creation is not spread evenly being dependent, as it is, on trade, raw materials, skills and craft. As I shall argue in Chapter 4, economic development occurs in real places, mainly cities, city regions and resource regions.

In previous waves, cities which came to have a golden age of prosperity are those who were positioned to take advantage of the new industries, either because of their existing status as entrepôts, because a new technology was invented there, because a new generation of entrepreneurs were at hand or because a tradition of innovation and enterprise was maintained even during the preceding depression. Thus, Manchester and cotton, Glasgow and ship-building, Pittsburgh and steel, Detroit and automobiles, Bristol and Seattle and aerospace, Silicon Valley and semi-conductors, Tokyo and consumer electronics, Helsinki and mobile phones,

Seattle and software. All of the great cities have come to prominence during growth periods. These include Edinburgh and Birmingham in the late eighteenth century, London and Paris in the early nineteenth century, Detroit, Birmingham and Stuttgart in the late nineteenth century, New York, LA and San Francisco in the mid-twentieth century, and most recently Seattle, Austin and Bangalore.

The rise of these cities historically is thus closely linked to the very intellectual and technological developments which gave rise to the great industries of each age. In fact, a similar dynamic – between the economic development of specific industries and the rise to prominence of certain cities – can be traced back to the Florence of the fourteenth century (wool and clothing), and Amsterdam and London in the seventeenth century (commodities such as spices, tea, coffee). The 'golden age' of most cities is associated with a particular episode of growth and wealth creation.

During these waves of economic development, cities themselves grow, that is to say they experience rapid population growth. This is usually accompanied by rising densities, surges in land values, pressures to expand into the surrounding countryside and a pattern of property booms. Very often, the pressures brought to bear result in calls for planned expansions of the city. This occurred in London and Paris in the eighteenth and nineteenth centuries, in Edinburgh in the 1770s, in the expansions of Barcelona, Amsterdam and Copenhagen, and in the planning of new American and Australian cities.

Commentary

It is only fair to acknowledge that many economists are today suspicious of long wave theory, on the not unreasonable grounds that it is unwise to read off current and future economic events on the basis of past trends. This is undoubtedly true. Yet, just as the seasons operate in cycles, as does the earth's climate, so too – it appears – does the process of wealth creation. Whatever the reason, economies grow in fits and starts, booms and busts, and not simply 'random walks'.[16]

Having acknowledged this point, there is now a significant body of scholarship on the long waves or K-waves.[17] Indeed, they continue to be referred to by

---

16 A random walk is the effect of plotting movements in share prices against all previous prices.

17 See in particular Rostow, W. W., *The Stages of Economic Growth* (Cambridge: Cambridge University Press, 1990); Hall, P. and Preston, P., *The Carrier Wave: New Information Technology and the Geography of Innovation* (London: Unwin Hyman, 1988); Berry, B. J. L., *Long-Wave Rhythms in Economic Development and Political Behavior* (Baltimore: Johns Hopkins University Press, 1991); Mensch, G., *Stalemate in Technology: Innovations Overcome the Depression* (Cambridge, MA: Ballinger, 1979); Modelski, G. and Thompson, W. R., *Globalization as an Evolutionary Process* (London: Taylor and Francis, 1996); Clark, J., Freeman, C. and Soete, L., 'Long Waves, Inventions, and Innovations', *Futures*, 15, 1981; Freeman, C. and Soete, L., *The Economics of Industrial Innovation*

economic think tanks and merchant banks in their confidential reports.[18] John Maynard Keynes also acknowledged the long waves in his *Treatise on Money* (1930):

> In the area of fixed capital it is easy to understand why fluctuations should occur in the rate of investment. Entrepreneurs are induced to embark on the production of fixed capital, or are deterred from doing so by their expectations of the profits to be made. Apart from the many minor reasons why these should fluctuate in a changing world, Professor Schumpeter's explanation of major movements may unreservedly be accepted. (p. 85)

What this means is that we cannot fully understand the workings of an economy by relying simply on what economists call 'constrained optimisation theory', or simple, everyday tracking of supply and demand. Traditional neo-classical economics is unable to foresee large fluctuations in an economy because it cannot factor in long-wave business cycles or indeed macroeconomic fluctuations over time. The recession or at least a downturn in 2009 was entirely foreseeable, and so too, for that matter, was the 'Credit Crunch'.

In this at least, Schumpeter, Keynes and Hayek were in agreement. Where Keynes saw 'animal spirits' or 'the will to action in preference to inaction' as the motivation for people's personal economic behaviour, Schumpeter saw a process of 'creative destruction' where the old generation is supplanted by the new. Hayek saw the problem as one of 'knowledge coordination'. All three saw that the problem with neo-classical economics based on 'rational choice' – as expounded for example by Paul Samuelson and Kenneth Arrow – is that people cannot have full knowledge and that where rational decisions are made on the bases of belief systems or hoped-for outcomes (gambling is the extreme example) individual behaviour can appear and is often irrational. Thus, if you believe the boom will continue through 1929 and into the 1930s, there is little I can do to change your mind. In such circumstances and conditions, at any one time an economy is made up of the actions of rational people acting rationally, and rational people acting irrationally (so far as the economic system is concerned).

Figure 2.4 reveals as much, plotting 20-year annualised growth rates for the United Kingdom.[19] What is striking about this is how close the data recorded by Angus Maddison is to Beckman's chart in Figure 2.1 for the period 1889 to 1984. Beckman, of course, developed his charts from a study of stock prices. Maddison's

---

(Cambridge, MA: MIT Press, 1997); Kleinknecht, A., *Innovation Patterns in Crisis and Prosperity: Schumpeter's Long Cycle Reconsidered* (London: Macmillan, 1987).

18   For example: Mager, Nathan H., The Kondratieff Waves (New York: Praeger, 1987), and a four-part series by Ralph D. Cato that was published in *Futures: The Magazine of Commodities*, March–June 1986.

19   Angus Maddison, formerly of the OECD, is now Emeritus Professor at the University of Groningen.

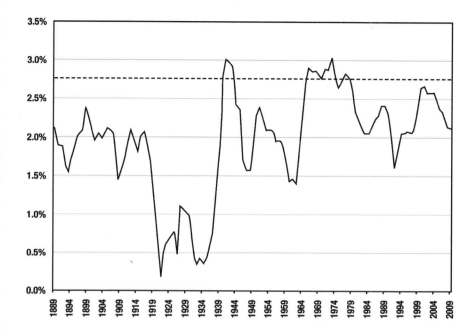

Figure 2.4 UK 20-year annualised growth rates

graph shows the collapse in growth in 1920, the stock market crash of 1929 and the Depression of the 1930s (until 1939). The growth phase of the 1950s is also visible, as it the recession of 1958/1959, followed by growth spurt of the 1960s and the peak of the last upwave in 1973. What is also interesting in Maddison's graph is that he is able to show the 'secondary prosperity' of the early 1980s, Black Monday in 1987, and the recession of the early 1990s. What appears to be the dot. com boom shows up in the late 1990s, and then what I refer to as the start of the next upwave, from about 2000–2002. The 2008–2009 recession can, on the chart, be compared to the tightening after the 'Wool Inflation' in 1952–1954.

The four previous K-waves have all involved a period of slow start-up, followed by fast growth, and ultimate levelling-off. The start-up period of each subsequent wave is characterised by flattening growth rates, declining profits, and severe competition within the previous lead industries. This period is known as the downswing or downwave. The K-waves are caused by the demand for solutions to new problems, and the supply of such solutions by innovative firms and inventors. Each wave alters economic geography. Britain's cotton wave was centred on Manchester. The 'information' K-wave developed from such locations as Silicon Valley and Orange County in California, and in Seattle. Each wave thus has its own specialisation but each in its own way changes the structure of the world economy. The fifth wave is now entering its phase of rapid economic growth, the upswing or upwave.

Chapter 3
The Problem with Economics

*In the beginning God made morons ... Then he got down to the task of making
complete imbeciles ... He placed a group of people on this planet who shared
the profound belief that wealth could be created in a vacuum.*

Robert Beckman, *The Downwave*, 1983

Supply and Demand

The gloomy science of economics, in the modern sense, began with the publication
of *The Wealth of Nations*, in three parts, by Adam Smith in the 1770s.[1] Smith
argued that economics is the study of the production, distribution, exchange and
consumption of goods and services under a system of markets for those goods
and services. He supported his arguments by examining not only his new concept
of the division of labour, but also the pricing of commodities, wages of labour,
rent, the origins and uses of money, the accumulation of capital, interest and the
division of stocks and shares. This has come to be known as classical economics,
concerned as it is with market conditions, supply and demand, commodity prices,
wage rates, interest and rent. Businesses compete with each other to provide goods
and services to satisfy consumer needs and aspirations, expressed as consumer
demand. This set of relationships underpins all forms of wealth creation, and is the
most dynamic system of economic development in history. Smith demonstrated
that wealth is created by people taking raw materials or existing goods and
applying their labour to create something other people want to buy.

Smith argued that it was this process that led to wealth creation and
improvements in prosperity. Smith saw that the more complex an economy's
'division of labour', the more wealth would tend to be created. Where Smith was
mistaken was to assume that the division of labour would of itself lead to greater
wealth creation. As Jane Jacobs reminded us, this is only the case if the labour so
organised is producing 'new work' that has a value in exchange.[2]

Smith, as a moral philosopher, was also interested in the question of how wealth
gets distributed. He famously used the metaphor of an invisible hand whereby an
economic actor is led to 'promote an end which was no part of his intention'. This
metaphor has been repeatedly misinterpreted, often deliberately, to suggest Smith
was referring to God. What he was saying, in fact, was that the rational actions

---

1   Smith, A., *The Wealth of Nations* (London: Penguin Classics, 1986; originally
published 1776).

2   Jacobs, J., *Cities and the Wealth of Nations* (New York: Random House, 1984).

of individuals in producing a good or service for sale, coupled with competition and market prices, leads to beneficial outcomes for society as a whole. Smith saw that markets deliver the fairest distribution of goods and services. This is what economists call 'efficiency', where outcomes are achieved to improve everyone's welfare, and the actors immediately concerned exchange at agreed prices. He wrote: 'It is not from the benevolence of the butcher, brewer or baker that we expect our dinner, but from regard to their own interest.'[3]

And so, Smith explained, prices operate as the key mechanism in a market: if there is too little supply for the level of demand, prices rise, producers increase production and consumers may consume less. If there is too much supply, prices fall, producers cut back production and consumers have less to buy. Prices thus fluctuate according to supply and demand, but tend to average out as markets mature. In sum, competitive markets and prices are what are required to achieve efficient outcomes.

Smith's model is still applied today, even although it tends to be considered within a framework that also contains macroeconomics (the largely ill-informed quest for equilibrium in the economy by balancing unemployment against inflation) and monetary policy (the control of the money supply to prevent governments printing paper money of declining value). Classical economics is central to our understanding of competition, industry sectors, and the ups and downs of commodity prices.

Smith's elegant formulations, studded and interwoven as they were with his keen observation of human behaviour and his philosophical interest in morality and the good society,[4] were unfortunately ousted by the rise of 'scientific' economists.

Mathematical Modelling

Adam Smith had provided a compelling account of how markets work to balance the needs of consumers with the economics of production. Jacques Turgot, meanwhile, formulated the 'law of diminishing returns', which demonstrates that producers will only continue to increase production up to the point where the rate of return makes their efforts futile.[5] On what became known as the demand side, Jeremy Bentham came up with the concept of 'utility' – the amount of pleasure or enjoyment derived from consuming a unit of some good or service – to explain the limits to people buying more than they need. There then developed, especially in nineteenth-century Britain, a view that society should be organised to balance out and ensure maximum utility or happiness. Adherents to this view called themselves

---

3   Smith, A. *The Wealth of Nations* (London: Penguin Classics, 1986; originally published 1776), p. 15.

4   Smith, A., *Theory of Moral Sentiments* (London: Prometheus, 2000).

5   Turgot is celebrated more often as a leading proponent of laissez-faire, the view that governments should minimise intervention in markets.

'Utilitarians', and the Whig and Liberal governments of Lord Melbourne, Lord Russell, Lord Palmerston and Gladstone effectively tried to run the British Empire as a Utilitarian project.[6] Economists, ever helpful, decided that they could assist in this by quantifying the costs and benefits of any decision. To do this, they applied mathematics and scientific method. Leading economists of what became known as the 'Marginalist'[7] era included Leon Walras, who set about the task of making economic systems predictable, so that supply and demand could be maintained in balance or 'in equilibrium'. Imagine this as a sort of seesaw: if prices go up too fast, the economy should be slowed and unemployment will increase; but if prices fall and unemployment increases, then the economy should be 'reflated' and prices will increase again.

This means smoothing out price fluctuations, and organising supply and demand to synchronise with each other. Walras derived the concept of 'equilibrium' from physics, and concluded that it ought to be possible, for any given economic system, to find a true point of equilibrium and therefore the true price of goods and services. By applying sophisticated mathematical models, Walras maintained, it is possible to predict how markets trade and equilibrium prices in an economy. But two fundamental errors had been committed: one, that dynamic systems such as economies should be pegged at a level of 'equilibrium'; and, two, that mathematical modelling was the means to achieve this. Nevertheless, the way was open for Utilitarians and economists such as William Stanley Jevons[8] to manipulate markets to achieve the 'best of all possible worlds'.

An entire new field of study evolved at the end of the nineteenth century and into the twentieth. Alfred Marshall[9] famously invented the supply and demand curve graphs. By the 1930s and 1940s, neo-classical economics as it became known, was ascendant. This involved the application of mathematical modelling to map the outcome of consumer 'preferences', as advocated by Paul Samuelson. Samuelson assumed that people make choices based on their preferences and that they act rationally in doing so. This was the beginnings of rational choice theory. Kenneth Arrow would argue that prices act to send signals in a market, to consumers and producers alike, and that therefore rational decision-making would drive the economic system to its equilibrium point of maximum social benefit. And so it would be possible to map economic trends and outcomes by studying price 'signals'.

---

6   Ferguson, N., *Empire: How Britain Made the Modern World* (London: Penguin, 2004).

7   See Beinhocker, E., *The Origin of Wealth* (London: Random House, 2007), Chapter 2, for more detail on the history of economic theory.

8   Jevons applied the physics of gravity and magnetic attraction to Bentham's concept of utility.

9   Marshall also developed the concept of 'agglomeration economies' to explain the benefits of firms and industries co-locating.

By the end of the twentieth century, the tenets of neo-classical or 'Traditional Economics' held sway, based on notions of 'optimising' consumers and producers making choices based on their preferences, these choices being 'bounded' by decreasing returns. The theory is that it is possible and desirable to manipulate economies to achieve optimal equilibrium, by influencing prices and thus supply and demand. Smith's brilliant insights had morphed into an industry.

Demand Management

During the 1930s, John Maynard Keynes argued that governments should intervene to correct economic instability and apparently believed that precisely defined amounts of fiscal stimulus or dampening would yield predictable and quantifiable results.[10] Here was another variation on Walras's idea of system equilibrium. This meant, happily, that unemployment could be traded off against inflation and the economy could be effectively and efficiently managed. Keynes was concerned to understand why there should be a Great Depression, and what could be done to lower unemployment. He followed Marx, to some extent, in the view that capitalism is subject to periodic crises caused by a collapse in demand.

Keynes recommended large-scale government spending to stimulate the demand side of the economy. He even suggested burying money in bottles and paying people to dig these up! Notwithstanding, Keynesianism seemed to work for a while, except in the United States where the recovery floundered under the New Deal.

The problem with New Deal style stimuli is that they do not work; and they often also cause inflation (the decline in value of currencies) as opposed to modest price fluctuations such as those in 2006–2007. There is compelling evidence[11] that the New Deal made the Great Depression deeper and longer lasting than it ought to have been. This is attributed to the killing off of competition through price fixing, high prescribed wage rates, high taxation and low levels of investment. Unemployment was still as high as 20 per cent in the United States in 1938. Some improvement was made through war production, paid for by the British, but the US economy only really recovered in the late 1940s. By 1946 inflation was approaching 20 per cent as the economy struggled to switch to non-war production. The next cycle of economic growth did not really kick in until 1948 as peacetime economies began once more to invest and produce. In this way, the Great Depression lasted not 10 years, but closer to 15 and even 20.

During the 1950s and 1960s governments sought to maintain economic growth and price stability through a combination of exchange rate stability and trade

---

10   Keynes, J. M., *The General Theory of Employment, Interest and Money* (London: Macmillan, 1936).

11   Cole, H. L. and Ohanian, L. E., 'New Deal Prolonged the Great Depression', *The Australian*, 5 February 2009.

liberalisation. This was the means by which Keynesian Demand Management would operate within the framework set down by the Bretton Woods agreement of 1948. The theory was that aggregate levels of demand and hence output and unemployment could be managed by 'fine-tuning' of taxation and government spending. When demand was too low, governments would cut taxes or increase spending; when too high, spending would be cut and taxes raised. Inflation was viewed as a serious problem, and so policy was 'tightened' in 1952 and 1958, causing recessions. Growth was choked off just as it was gaining a head of steam. By about 1960 it was clear that demand management, rather than smoothing out curves in the economic cycle, was making matters worse. Interventions tended to be too late and there were numerous currency crises caused by large imbalances in the balance of payments in many countries. As early as 1961, the Macmillan government in the UK was in the midst of a 'great reappraisal' of the tenets of Keynesian demand management.

The problem was that the Bretton Woods fixed exchange rates could only be maintained by central banks buying and selling currency. If the value of sterling was too high, then the Bank of England sold it to bring down the price; if too low, the Bank would purchase sterling with its reserves of other currencies. But if the balance of trade was in the red, then the Bank's stock of foreign currencies would dwindle, and so its room for manoeuvre became limited. This explains why British economists of the day were calling for a devaluation of sterling.

The emergence of stagflation after 1973 came as something of a shock. Here was proof concrete that the unthinkable was possible: economies can experience high unemployment and high inflation at the same time. Keynesianism had no answer to stagflation; there was no comfortable trade-off between inflation and unemployment, no neat see-saw that could be managed. All of this gives the lie to the famous Phillips curve[12] that counter-poses the level of unemployment *against* the inflation rate. The curve purports to show that the pressure of demand in an economy causes inflation since, as unemployment falls in times of higher growth, workers demand higher wages and thus trigger wage inflation. The Phillips curves were quietly forgotten in the 1970s when low growth and high inflation were shown to co-exist.

Nevertheless, their central tenet that growth must be balanced against inflation still holds sway in central banks around the world. Many government economists still argue today that the jobless rate in an economy cannot be allowed to drop too far as this will of itself produce inflation. Known, sophistically, as the 'Non-Accelerating Inflation Rate of Unemployment', this consigns people to the dole (where a lot of them are quite happy, it must be admitted) at a time of labour *shortages*.

---

12   The Phillips curve was developed by A. W. H. Phillips, a professor at the London School of Economics in the 1950s. Phillips later rejected the view that his curve represented a theory of the causes of inflation.

A similar observation was made by the noted economist and expert in the Phillips curve, Dr Arthur Okun. Okun came to reject what by this time was conventional theory, arguing that putting unemployment up to reduce inflation makes no sense; indeed, it makes things worse. He went on to propose[13] a 'discomfort index', combining both inflation and unemployment – similar to the heat and humidity index used by meteorologists. At the time, inflation was around 7 per cent and unemployment 5 per cent, giving a total of 12 per cent. Okun argued that lowering inflation to 4 per cent by increasing unemployment to 10 per cent would increase the 'discomfort index'.

The problem, of course, is one of low growth producing both unemployment and inflation. Once an economy loses dynamism, the likelihood is that unemployment will continue to rise and so too will prices if goods become less available. Jane Jacobs pointed out[14] that very high prices are very often found in backward or under-performing economies, such as Portugal in the 1970s (then a military dictatorship) or Scotland in the eighteenth century. High unemployment and high inflation, far from being opposite ends of a see-saw, often co-exist. As Matthews pointed out in the late 1960s,[15] the 'golden age' of the 1950s and 1960s was not due to Keynesian demand management at all, but rather to the post-war surge in private investment or what he called 'a very substantial arrears of investment opportunities'. In other words: investment, profitability, innovation and enterprise.

Monetarism

Keynesianism was largely abandoned during the 1970s and 1980s, to be replaced by a new economic orthodoxy, Monetarism. This argued that levels of growth, employment and inflation in the economy can be manipulated by adjustments to interest rates and hence the cost of credit and the overall supply of money. To stimulate growth, interest rates are lowered; to lower inflation, interest rates are raised.

This followed from John Stuart Mill's observation a century earlier that expansion or contraction of credit advanced to producers was key to economic expansion. In other words, an increased supply of money would lead to growth. This new theory was labelled Monetarism and its leading proponent was Milton Friedman following Irving Fisher. Fisher had earlier argued that the Great Depression was caused by a drastic contraction of credit as banks stopped lending. Fisher proposed that the way to overcome the Depression should have been to

---

13   Arthur Okun was an economic advisor to President Lyndon B. Johnson. His 'discomfort index' is discussed in Jacobs, J., *Cities and the Wealth of Nations* (New York: Random House, 1984).

14   Ibid.

15   Matthews, R. C. O., 'Why has Britain had Full Employment since the War?', *The Economic Journal*, 1968.

expand credit to producers and over time stabilise the volume of bank credit. This could be done by government control of money supply.[16]

It would take governments in the UK, United States and later Europe nearly 50 years to follow Fisher's prescriptions, but once Keynesianism had failed Monetarism was king. Now, instead of demand management, the economy could be managed by manipulating interest rates and therefore the uptake of credit. To attack inflation, put interest rates up and increase the cost of money; to attack unemployment, cut interest rates. These measures could also be supported by lowering or increasing tax rates, but only if government spending could likewise be varied. Economic management since the 1980s has largely been based on interest rate policy. The problem remains, however, that putting rates up too far penalises producers and the labour force, while cutting them too far is held to be responsible for inflation.

Yet, in Milton Friedman's view inflation is almost always caused by governments printing money, that is expanding the 'money supply'. He once remarked that 'inflation is the one form of taxation that can be imposed without legislation'. Those who pay the price are ordinary families, pensioners on fixed incomes and people with savings. Friedman must be spinning in his grave.

Yet it remains possible to have high unemployment and high inflation at the same time, or low unemployment and low inflation. How can this be so? Some monetarists argue that there exists a 'natural unemployment rate' and that if this is high then inflation and unemployment can co-exist even though the theory of price stability says otherwise. It seems more likely to me that it is the theory that is wrong rather than the real world. This would mean, for example, that the stagflation of previous recessions and depressions could return again as it seems clear that high inflation accompanies high unemployment under conditions of stagnation and economic decline.

Take the period since 2000. Interest rates had been lowered somewhat in response to the dot.com bust and the Asian collapse. Following 9/11, rates were cut drastically in an effort to ward off recession. This may seem perfectly understandable, but the truth is that rates were cut too far, resulting in a surge in debt. On the plus side, economic growth was maintained in the advanced capitalist economies at a modestly healthy rate of about 3 per cent per annum. But by 2006 central bankers began to worry about rising 'inflation', even although we can now see that these were simply price increases for goods affected by droughts and oil prices. In order to reduce inflation, base rates were raised sharply over a short period of time. The US Federal Reserve governor Alan Greenspan and his successor Ben Bernanke ignored warnings that this sort of drastic over-correction would trigger a marked slowdown. As we now know, it also triggered large-scale defaulting on mortgage payments, the collapse of the US housing market and the banking panic.

---

16   Fisher, I., *100% Money* (New York: Adelphi Company, 1934).

If indeed Monetarism is the best that can be done, then it is not a vast improvement on demand management. The temptation to 'act' seems to accentuate rather than temper the cycle of boom and bust. It might be better for us all if regulators did more watching and understanding than intervening over-zealously. The problem with economic growth is that it is too complex for any simplistic theory to comprehend. The recent history of monetary policy around the world – certainly in the United States, UK, Europe and Australia – has been problematic, to say the least. The economic slowdown and recession of 2008/2009 occurred because of, rather than despite, monetary policy. The biggest problem – aside from the fact that it is impossible to achieve an equilibrium in dynamic economies – is the fear of inflation.

The Austrians

The Austrian School (also known as the Vienna School or the Psychological School[17]) came to prominence through the work of Hayek, Mises and Rothbard. The Austrians see themselves as resurrecting the classical liberal (not neo-classical) tenets of the French Scholastic Tradition, economists such as Turgot, Robert Cantillon and Jean Baptiste Say. Cantillon understood the market as an entrepreneurial process, such that growth in the economy develops in a step-by-step fashion, disrupting prices along the way. Say famously argued – Say's Law – that economies can never over-produce on a sustained basis as prices would readjust both supply and demand. Turgot favoured minimal government intervention.

Austrian School economists likewise advocate minimal government intervention in economies. The Austrian School was influential in the early twentieth century when their theory of subjective value, based on individual preferences, was taken up by neo-classical economists. The Austrians accept the centrality of prices in economic systems, but they argue that the complexity of human behaviour makes mathematical modelling of the evolving market extremely difficult, not to say impossible. This view is now shared by many economic 'behaviouralists' such as James Buchanan.

During the 1920s and 1930s, Hayek and Mises authored many studies on the business cycle, warned of the danger of credit expansion, and predicted the Great Depression. Hayek later became a prime opponent of Keynesian economics with books on exchange rates, capital theory and monetary reform. Rothbard published an investigation of the Great Depression, which applied Austrian business cycle theory to show that the stock market crash and economic downturn was attributable to a prior bank credit expansion. This has become perhaps the central tenet of Austrian School economic theory, that governments should not encourage

---

17   Most of the founding fathers of the Austrian School were Austrians. Many of them fled Austria and Germany in the 1930s and 1940s, taking up residency in Britain and the United States.

credit expansion by artificially lowering interest rates. They would argue that the severity of the recession in 2009 was triggered by the 'Credit Crunch', itself caused by artificially low interest rates and reckless lending.

The Inflation Bogey

Early in 2008, the word 'inflation' was being bandied about like confetti at a mafia wedding. 'Fighting the Inflation Challenge' in Australia involved cumulative increases in interest rates during 2005, 2006 and 2007. The official headline rate of inflation in Australia, in December 2007, was running at just over 3 per cent per annum, broadly in line with the Euro-zone, the UK and United States. After 11 years of slow recovery from the low point of 1992, the Australian economy and stock market was self-evidently booming only from 2004. This is largely credited to a surge in demand from China and India for Australian coal, minerals and wheat.

In March 2006, Tropical Cyclone Larry devastated Queensland's banana crop. This caused a severe shortage of bananas, imports of which are strictly limited. The price of bananas increased sharply, from $3 per kilogram to $12 per kilogram, so of course people stopped buying them. In this way, the rise in the price of bananas would be self-correcting. But, at the Federal Reserve Bank, the rising cost of bananas was seen as inflationary, even if they were left to rot on the frond. And so interest rates were increased in order to lower this fruit-driven inflation. The inflation in this case, assuming the average family eats a bunch of bananas each week, would be some $450 per year.

Shortly thereafter, increased oil prices internationally forced up the costs of petrol and therefore transport costs. This prompted the Federal Reserve to increase interest rates again, even although their own data revealed that most of the food price increases at the time were because of increased transport costs – the average basket of vegetables increased from about $10 per week to $15 – and the effects of the long drought on agricultural production. Wheat prices, for example, rose over 160 per cent in 2007. Bread increased from $1 a loaf to $1.70, about $500 over the year. There is nothing much the consumer can do about this except buy less bread, fruit and *legumes*. So far, in 2006, the average Australian household was some $900 per annum worse off in the purchase of fruit and vegetables and bread. Petrol price increases around this time added another $1,000 per annum to the household expenditure.

By the second half of 2007, price increases were still seen as a worry, but this time the largest increases were in the cost of housing following earlier interest rate hikes. Mortgage repayments were now costing substantially more because of official policy. In Australia this has a rapid knock-on effect in the residential rental market as a large proportion of the stock is owned by individuals as 'investment properties' and purchased on mortgages. If the increase in housing costs is seen as inflationary, then putting up interest rates is a sure-fire way of stoking the flames. If we assume an average mortgage of $250,000, then an increase from 6 per cent to 8 per cent interest produces an additional annual cost of $5,000. Inflation then becomes a self-fulfilling prophecy.

By December 2007, the costs of food were actually falling – they were self-correcting because people would not pay the higher prices at the supermarket. Meanwhile, the price of electronic goods continued to fall, as they always have done, because market competition brings more producers into the market. But, and it is a big but, government charges suddenly began to rise – local rates and transport costs especially – 'to keep up with inflation'. Again, there were increases for petrol, bank charges, energy and housing costs. Australia's inflation, in early 2008, was now largely a product of *putting up interest rates*. Undaunted, the Federal Reserve made two more interest rate rises in 2008.

It seems to me that there is a serious misconception about what inflation is and its role in economic development. The orthodox view, according to Traditional Economics, is that inflation is caused by an imbalance of supply and demand such that too much money chases too few goods, but this has not occurred in Australia – even for bananas, as we have seen. Or inflation is caused, according to Monetarists – by governments printing paper of money of declining value – but this has not occurred either, indeed the Aussie dollar has steadily been increasing in value (to the extent where exporters and the tourist industry are beginning to howl in pain). So none of these 'demand-pull' factors seems to have been at work at all. Undeterred, the Federal Reserve promised 'more pain'. But if food prices were declining (even bananas), if the main sources of rising prices were bank fees and mortgage repayments, then what exactly was the point in raising interest rates? Putting the price of housing up seems a rather convoluted way to attempt control of petrol prices.

Historically, it has been the case (since the early 1800s at least) that rises in prices accompany growth and economic development. Thus in the United States, we find that average annual inflation was 8.7 per cent from 1913 to 1919, fell to zero in the 1920s and was negative during the 1930s. Inflation picked up again in the 1940s at an annual average of 5.63 per cent, settled down to between 2 per cent and 3 per cent for the 1950s and 1960s, before surging again (7.09 per cent) during the 1970s. It fell slowly throughout the early 1980s, almost to zero in the early 1990s and was only about 2–3 per cent in 2007. Peaks occurred in 1956, 1961, 1974, 1979 and 1990. Periods of inflation, or more precisely rising prices, certainly occur in times of rapid economic expansion, for example in the 1900s and in the late 1940s.

But the *highest* peaks occur as the economy moves into a period of low growth when, indeed, there is too much money chasing too few goods or too few sound investments. In the UK, inflation peaked at 25 per cent in 1975, at a time of economic contraction. This resulted in 'stagflation', leading ultimately to Black Monday in October 1987 and the 1990s recession. By contrast, periods of high economic growth such as the 1950s tend to have inflation at about the 2–3 per cent mark, or 3–4 per cent in the UK at that time. Harold Macmillan, the British Prime

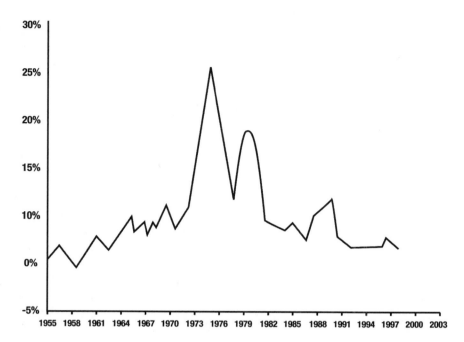

Figure 3.1 Inflation in five countries

Minister at the time, remarked in 1956 that fighting inflation was his top priority, but then quietly set about expanding the economy instead.

It seems, then, that inflation occurs in different forms and for differing reasons. When the economy is growing well, price increases of 2–3 per cent are probably the minimum one should expect, a sort of 'natural' level of inflation or white noise. In any event, in the absence of external shocks – a sudden increase in oil prices or a drought for example – rising prices tend to correct themselves. However, where levels of return and economic growth drop suddenly, as in the 1920s or 1970s, much higher rates of inflation will follow. Finally, there is super-inflation of the sort that afflicted the Weimar Republic in Germany in the early 1920s or Argentina in the 1990s or Zimbabwe today. This is an altogether different phenomenon that comes about when the productive economy collapses and with it the value of money.

As for wage inflation and price increases brought about by 'capacity constraints' or skill shortages, these are secondary phenomena that, during economic upwaves, follow rather than lead other price increases. Thus, a shortage of labour is a consequence of economic growth, not the other way round. Similarly infrastructure blockages or the need to expand floorspace or to invest in machinery are also largely self-correcting in that firms and collaborative ventures will tend to respond to market data by investing in new facilities or transit systems. Government investment in airports, seaports, rail and road is also important, provided the project in question is necessary, is targeted at overall economic growth and is built in the right place at the right time.

To put this forward as an economic 'model', I propose there are four types of inflation or price rises (I have based this on the observation that not all forms of certain infectious diseases are considered equally worrisome, for example Hepatitis A, B and C):

- Type A: where prices increase at a normal rate in line with fluctuations in supply and demand. This is a normal part of economic life that occurs during times of economic growth. The policy response should be to sit tight to allow prices time to correct.
- Type B: where prices increase because of sudden external shocks to ongoing economic life, for example a sudden hike in oil prices or a severe drought. Again the policy response should be to wait and see if the oil price will fall; if not fuel duty should be cut as an *anti-inflation* measure.
- Type C: where the productive economy slows to the point of stagnation producing both higher prices (goods are in fewer supply) and high unemployment. This is known as stagflation, and it occurs as the business cycle moves into a period of deep and prolonged recession such as in the 1970s or the 1930s.
- Type D: hyper-inflation occurs when economic collapse is complete and the value of money is a meaningless concept.

By assuming that all price increases are inflation, policy-makers fail to see that most price increases are both a necessary condition and a consequence of wealth creation, and are, moreover, largely self-correcting. More dangerous forms of inflation occur only at particular times in the business cycle and are symptoms not of growth but precipitous decline. Current interest rate policy fails to distinguish between price increases that are part and parcel of economic dynamism, those that are self-correcting and those where price increases are indeed inflationary. Because of this, measures taken to increase interest rates are usually counter-productive: they make matters worse. The problem is that both Monetarist and Keynesian models of inflation are based upon a fallacy, because, simply put, not all price increases are 'inflation'.

Banking Collapses

Bank collapses, though worrying, are nothing new. They have happened frequently in the past, and will happen again. Problems arise when unsecured loans are made to unsuitable borrowers, and when banks then trade loans and other accounts (bonds, stocks, mortgages) with each other. This leads to a form of pyramid selling, inevitably leading to a collapse of some form. There is a distinction to be made, however, between banking collapses that follow share collapses, as in 1929, and those that occur when broad economic conditions are reasonably sound. The problem is almost always triggered when banks stray from their primary purpose, to lend and borrow money, to indulge in social engineering or social projects deemed beneficial in the politics of the day. Take the example of the Ayr Bank.

In 1772 the collapse of the Ayr Bank led to the Edinburgh banking crisis of that year, and also led to tremors amongst London banks. Only three of Edinburgh's 30 private banks survived. Adam Smith commented that 'the operations of this bank seem to have produced effects quite opposite from what was intended'.[18] The Ayr Bank had been established in 1770 to provide long-term loans and provide credit to people who otherwise found it difficult to borrow. The bank granted cash accounts and loaned people 100 per cent of the costs of their specific projects. Interest rates were set at 5 per cent. The Ayr Bank borrowed from other banks in London and Edinburgh to raise the capital it would loan to others. As borrowers began to default, or were otherwise tardy in making repayments, the Bank had to pay off its debts to London banks by securing greater loans. This state of affairs was clearly unstable.

Smith compared the banking collapse to the Mississippi Bubble of 1716–1720, 'a scheme of fraudulent debtors to cheat their creditors'. This, the brainchild of another Scot, John Laws, was a scheme to develop France's possessions in North America backed by paper money and credit. As people bought shares in the new currency, its value increased. The demand for credit rose dramatically as people sought a share of the promised new wealth, pledging their homes and possessions as security. The Mississippi Company collapsed in 1720, taking with it the entire banking and credit system of France. A combination of greed, an over-extension of credit and unreal expectations was to blame. Smith saw that the role played by the Ayr Bank was similar, advancing as it did credit to finance a speculative boom in housing, turnpikes and canals, the 'transport infrastructure' of the time. Smith's final verdict on the Ayr Bank collapse was that it only enabled borrowers 'to get into much deeper in to debt, so that when ruin came, it fell so much the heavier'.[19] The British economy struggled to recover from the banking crisis for another 10 years, that is until the 1780s.

Another example is the Commercial Crisis of 1857–1858, although in this case the economy of the time was growing strongly. The surge in credit was directed to building railways, and speculation in the prices of wheat and other commodities. The financial panic spread from the United States to Britain and on to Europe in a period of about 18 months. However, this time there was a strong recovery in economic growth, the great recession of the cycle not occurring until the 1880s and 1890s.

---

18   For Smith's view of the Ayr Bank, see *The Wealth of Nations* (London: Penguin Classics, 1986), pp. 412–17.

19   See O'Rourke, P. J., *On the New Wealth of Nations* (London: Allen & Unwin, 2007), p. 68.

During the 1840s, modern capitalism was growing strongly. Prices surged between 1852 and 1854, the good times had returned after the recession of 1830s and early 1840s.[20] The lead industries of the day were iron and steel, shipbuilding, railways and heavy engineering. The great powerhouses of production were Pittsburgh and Glasgow. In the United States, it was the great railway age and the opening up of the West; in Britain, Glasgow was the Second City of the Empire.[21] This great upwave of wealth creation peaked in about 1864 and was followed by a period of secondary prosperity, before plunging into the deep recession of the 1880s and early 1890s. During the upwave, there were one or two ups and downs, notably the Great Panic of 1857.

Panic in this sense refers to a collapse in confidence in banks and banking, and is often characterised by a rush of investors trying to get their money out of the banks. This run on the banks leads in turn to a rapid fall of the securities market, bank failures and bankruptcies as credit dries up. An overwhelming sense of foreboding ensues, a climate of fear. The Great Panic was caused at root by large-scale investment by European banks and investors in US railway bonds. Unfortunately for all concerned, the railway companies over-stretched themselves in buying up land and committing to too many infrastructure projects at once. They began to default on bond payments. This triggered a run and sharp decline in the value of railroad securities. The effects were fairly spectacular: the closing of banks, severe unemployment in the United States and a money-market panic across Europe.[22] The speed at which the Panic spread caused great surprise and concern, and was due to steamships and early telegraph lines. Because of this, the 1857 Panic is sometimes referred to as the 'first world-wide commercial crisis in the history of modern capitalism'.[23]

The Panic kicked off on 24 August 1857 with the collapse of the New York branch of the Ohio Life Assurance and Trust Company, an event that occasioned rioting in the streets. By 12 October that year, 62 of 63 of New York's commercial banks had suspended payments. In November 1857 the Panic had spread to Britain where the Bank Act of 1844 was suspended. This led to a financial panic across Northern Europe, especially in Austria. In Britain, there were a large number of bank failures, including the Western Bank of Scotland, the City of Glasgow Bank, Sanderson, Sandeman & Co. of London, the Wolverhampton and Staffordshire Bank and the Northumberland and District Bank.

---

20   Beckman, R., *The Downwave* (London: Pan Books, 1983).

21   Montgomery, J., *The New Wealth of Cities: City Dynamics and the Fifth Wave* (Aldershot: Ashgate, 2007).

22   Evans, D. M., *The History of the Commercial Crisis 1857–1858* (Newton Abbot: David and Charles, 1859).

23   Hughes, J. R. T., *The Commercial Crisis of 1857* (Oxford: Oxford University Press, 1956).

Contemporaries disagreed on the origin of the Panic.[24] Some blamed New York banks for making too many loans, some the withdrawal of funds by New York country banks, some pointed out that many of the loans advanced were bad risk, while the Banking Superintendent, a Mr James Cook, described the Panic as being 'without apparent reason'. Lawmakers in Britain blamed the crisis on 'excessive speculation and abuse of credit'[25] and greed. But when a more sober historical analysis was undertaken, this was found to be a 'somewhat superficial' explanation.[26] Hughes argues instead that the switch to investment in US railways followed a fall in profitability in the British domestic economy, an export boom and a switch to overseas investments, as well as a growth of banking and commercial credit or bank lending. Essentially the banks were extending credit to people wishing to buy US rail stocks, and also buying these stocks themselves. No one was expecting the railway stocks to fail. In this way, the Panic of 1857 follows a well-worn path, taken earlier during the Ayr Bank collapse of 1772, the Mississippi Bubble of 1720 and the South Sea Bubble of the early 1700s. The deal was too good to be true.

What was different about the Panic of 1857 was that it occurred during a period of rapid economic growth, rather than at the end of the boom/beginning of the depression. This means that banking collapses can occur even when the 'real' economy is strong, and this is what I believe has happened in 2008. As late as July 2008, the US economy had achieved 3 per cent annualised growth in the second quarter, and central banks around the world were putting up interest rates to ward off perceived inflation. The collapse of Lehman Brothers and the bailout of Fannie Mae in September 2008 came as a great surprise to most of us, including central bankers. This is because the collapse was not due to economic weakness but to pyramid selling of bad debt. Almost exactly the same as in 1857 and 1772.

The Sub-Prime Mortgage Panic

The early 1990s were the depth of the 1987–1993 recession followed by a decade of slow but steady growth.[27] The Japanese 'Bubble Economy' had burst in January 1990. The run on European currencies led by speculators such as George Soros occurred during 1993. But by 1995, the depths of the recession had been navigated.

24   Calomiris, C. W. and Schweikar, L., 'The Panic of 1857: Origins, Transmission and Containment', *Journal of Economic History*, 51(4), December 1991.

25   Report of the Select Committee on the Bank Acts and the Recent Commercial Distress, 1858.

26   Hughes, J. R. T., *The Commercial Crisis of 1857* (Oxford: Oxford University Press, 1956).

27   Western economies grew at roughly 1–2 per cent per annum, the boom kicking off in about 2004.

People began to feel wealthier and this helped underpin a property boom in the late 1990s through until about 2002.

Christopher Leinberger[28] explains the entry of Wall Street banks as big players in US real estate from the late 1980s. This was the time of the Saving and Loan banking crisis, when over 1,000 banks collapsed under the weight of risky loans made to property buyers. The residual loans were taken over by the Federal Deposit Insurance Corporation (FDC) in 1989, and later the Resolution Trust Corporation (RTC), which assumed title to billions of dollars of real estate assets. Difficult though this is to believe, it was only at this point that the Federal Reserve Bank and Wall Street realised that about one-third of all economic assets in the United States are in the form of real estate. The RTC then set about the task of selling off these assets at fire-sale prices, handily just in time for the economic recovery that kicked in around 1994. The real estate market surged from 1995.

Wall Street realised that there are rich pickings in property development, and set up Real Estate Investment Trusts (REITs) to bundle properties into larger groupings that people could invest in – a bit like Investment Trusts more generally. More than 80 such REITs were launched in 1993 alone, most of them comprised solely of formerly bankrupt real estate portfolios. Around the same time, Wall Street firms began trading in commercial mortgage-backed securities (CMBS), a business model pioneered by the Resolution Trade Corporation, a government agency. The secondary residential mortgage market also gained momentum at this time, another market that was created by the federal government in the mid 1980s and enthusiastically 'delivered' by Fannie Mae and Freddie Mac and their friends in merchant banks such as Lehman Brothers, Morgan Stanley, Merrill Lynch and the like. According to Prof. Leinberger, the REITs had a market capitalisation of $438 billion by the end of 2005, while the secondary residential market was $5.5 trillion and the CMBSs were $721 billion. Could this be an asset bubble, ripened to the point of bursting?

It was during the 1990s, also, that President Clinton instructed the Fannie Mae (The Federal National Mortgage Association) Corporation to ease credit requirements on loans to ethnic minorities and low-income earners. A nationwide scheme, the pilot programme alone involved 24 banks. This was to include what became known as the 'sub-prime sector'. Fannie Mae's chairman and chief executive in 1999 is quoted as saying that in addition to 'reducing down payment requirements' the corporation would underwrite loans in the sub-prime market.[29]

Fannie Mae and its sister corporation Freddie Mac are 'Government Sponsored Enterprises' (GSEs). This means that they are exempted from taxation and any losses are guaranteed by public monies, although shares of profits go overwhelmingly to investors, executives and board members with shares. This

---

28   Leinberger, C. B., *The Option of Urbanism: Investing in a New American Dream* (Washington: Island Press, 2008).

29   'Fannie Mae Eases Credit to Aid Mortgage Lending', *New York Times*, 30 September 1999.

is a hangover from its foundation in 1938 as a means to provide liquidity in the mortgage market that had collapsed following the Wall Street Crash of 1929.[30] The idea was to provide Federal money to local banks who would then finance home loans at below market interest rates.[31] Fannie Mae held a virtual monopoly of what became know as the US 'secondary mortgage market' until 1968 when Lyndon B. Johnson converted it into a private corporation or rather a 'government supported enterprise'. A second GSE, Freddie Mac (the Federal Home Mortgage Corporation) was established in 1970.[32]

It is important to realise that Fannie Mae does not lend money directly to consumers but rather it purchases loans that banks make on the secondary market. This was made possible by Fannie Mae being allowed, uniquely, to borrow money from overseas at low interest rates backed by the US government. Fannie Mae passed this on to borrowers in the form of low down payments and fixed rate mortgages. The parallels with the Ayr Bank are startling.

However, the strategy announced in 1999 was to spur the banks to make more loans to people with poor credit ratings, and especially to blacks and Hispanics. This was done by offering mortgages at 1 per cent above the standard variable rate. Homeownership rates amongst these groups had in fact been growing rapidly during the period 1993–1998, 87 per cent for Hispanics and 72 per cent for blacks, but this was considered insufficient to close the gap between these and other groups. As early as 1998, Fannie Mae was already making 44 per cent of its purchases from loans to these groups.

Not everyone at the time was convinced this was a good idea. Peter Wallison of the American Enterprise Institute warned that 'if they fail, the government will have to step up and bail them out'.[33] The US Senate Finance Committee in 2005 considered a bill to increase scrutiny of Fannie Mae and its accountancy mechanisms. In 2003 it had been revealed that Freddie Mac's accounting practices contained $4.5 billion worth of errors. By this time, combined debt at Freddie Mac and Fannie Mae was equal to 46 per cent of the then national debt.[34] The then head of the Reserve Bank, Alan Greenspan, warned of forthcoming financial collapse if Fannie Mae's activities were not reined in. The bill was opposed by the Democrats and lost.

The trigger that caused the bubble to burst was the raising of interest rates by the Federal Reserve in 2006 and 2007, to ward off a perceived risk of inflation. This sent mortgage payments 'through the roof' and hundreds of thousands of Fannie Mae's customers defaulted on their payments, walking away from their homes. With the collapse in the housing market came the collapse of Fannie Mae and the

---

30 Oddly, by 1938 the housing market was already recovering.
31 Alford, Rob, 'What are the Origins of Fannie Mae and Freddie Mac', History News Network, 2003.
32 The Nixon administration did this to prevent Fannie Mae becoming a monopoly!
33 *New York Times*, op. cit.
34 Alford, op. cit.

loans it had purchased from the banks. Before long, the banks were collapsing too, not all of them but those who had bought and sold sub-prime loans. Defaults by 2007 were running at just under 3 per cent of all mortgages in the United States. This seems a small proportion, but it represents hundreds of thousands of loans, and billions of dollars.

The culprits in all of this were the executives and board members of Fannie Mae for buying unsecured and risky loans, the Federal Reserve for putting up interest rates too far and too quickly, and the banks for what almost amounts to pyramid selling of bad debt, fools' mortgages. Fannie Mae's structural flaws were an accident waiting to happen. But there is another culprit. The Clinton administration, in pressuring Fannie Mae, created the policy of lending initially good and then bad money to people who were themselves bad credit risks. This was done, no doubt, for good political – not to say politically correct – reasons: the targeted extension of home ownership to minority groups. But it can now be seen that this sort of social engineering has been achieved at a heavy cost, not least to those who have lost their houses and taxpayers who may now have to pick up the cost of an emergency package. People who were awarded such loans may well be forgiven for thinking they are now worse off than they were in 1999.

The lesson of all of this is not that Wall Street is 'greedy', nor even that banks should be limited in the selling-on of debt, although periodically both of these observations are certainly true. The main lesson is that banking and credit should be run on sound banking principles rather than as a political project. For where politicians become involved in banking, as in the case of Democrats and Fannie Mae, only incompetence, pork-barrelling and even corruption will follow. As Adam Smith put it: 'I have never known much good done by those who affected to trade for the public good.'

The banking collapse of 2008 was not systemic, it was not caused by some sort of 'inherent greed' within capitalism. It was caused by bad lending, shonky financial products and the incompetence of Fannie Mae executives, their opposite numbers in the merchant banks, and politicians who failed in their oversight role. For railway bonds in 1857, read unsecured mortgages in 2008.

New Keynesianism

Some are now arguing that Monetarism was wrong all along, and what we need is a return to demand management and Keynesian economics.[35] Take for example, the case made for 'infrastructure investment' or public capital spending. The Keynesian argument is that this pumps money into the economy and helps fuel recovery and growth. This, the Left argues, was behind the success of the New Deal in the 1930s. But the New Deal was not a success: the recession was deep and

---

35   For example the *New York Times* columnist Paul Krugman, or the Labour politicians Ed Balls and Yvette Cooper in the UK.

lasted 15 years; it was the tooling up for the Second World War that ended the Great Depression, and the return of growth in the private sector in 1947. The New Deal actually made things worse. Unemployment in the United States peaked officially at 24.9 per cent in 1933 but remained at over 20 per cent for 1934 and 1935, falling slightly but still at 19 per cent in 1938. In the UK, by contrast, unemployment peaked at 22.1 per cent in 1931, after which it fell steadily to 10.8 per cent in 1937.

The New Deal ushered in extraordinary powers for government intervention usually reserved for wartime – the National Recovery Act (NRA). This set aside anti-trust laws (which ensure competition), raised prices and wages in cooperation with the unions, restricting output (to maintain prices) and placing quotas on investment in plant and equipment. This had the effect of depressing production and employment and therefore the recovery. The New Deal was to all intents a command economy. Over 500 industries were centrally planned under the NRA.

Of course, there were infrastructure projects carried out at this time, no doubt many of them a good thing, including the Hoover Dam and the Tennessee Valley Water Project. But they had little impact in reflating the economy in any immediate sense or even over 10 years. The reason for this is that of funds committed for any project, only about 25 per cent is spent in the early years of planning and engineering, say years one to three. Moreover, most of what is spent goes on materials and land rather than on the payroll. From about year three of any project, at best 35 per cent of spending will feed into the economy in the form of wages and salaries. So capital projects take a long time to get up and running, and their economic impact is less than 35 per cent of total spending. By the time a large project is completed, the recovery in the economy should already be well underway. Cutting taxes and interest rates is more straightforward and more immediate.

Even more worrying is where governments over-spend in stimulus measures or on welfare services more generally. If government spending grows too rapidly and beyond the means of the economy, borrowing will have to increase. Where this gets out of control, a 'Fiscal Crisis of the State' may ensue, where governments cannot meet debt repayments and are marked down as bad 'sovereign risks'. And this indeed is what is now happening in Greece, Ireland, Portugal, Spain and perhaps Italy.

'Solving' one problem thus causes another. And by the policy of 'quantitative easing' or printing money, governments may well reduce their debt problem, but at the cost of a rise in inflation, this time caused by lax money supply. Through its recent programme of quantitative easing, the Bank of England has printed an extra £200 billion. Towards the end of 2010, the US Federal Reserve created another $600 billion to add to the $1.7 trillion it had already pumped into the US monetary system. Central bankers in Britain and America are committed to the idea that prosperity can be printed. Martin Feldstein, professor of economics at Harvard, describes this as a 'dangerous gamble', while Germany's finance minister, Wolfgang Schäuble, branded it 'clueless'. At some point, in order to deal with the resultant inflation and asset bubbles, monetary policy will again be tightened, and by about 2018 there will be another mild recession. The pattern of boom and bust will continue, made worse not better by central intervention.

Commentary

Modern economics is now a strange amalgam of neo-Keynesianism, in the form of increased government expenditures, and Monetarism in the manipulation of inflation against growth by means of setting interest rates. Central banks are wedded to the idea that inflation and unemployment must be held in balance. Nevertheless, they are quite prepared to print money to get them out of the debt caused by over-spending and in dealing with the 'GFC'.

Indeed, this notion that there is a long-term 'sustainable' growth rate of an economy – where inflation and unemployment are balanced – lies at the heart of modern economics.[36] These days, this is referred to as 'trend growth', or average annual increases in GDP.[37] Oddly enough, the UK trendsetters only go back as far as 1989 in constructing their models. This misses out such key events in economic history as the 1973 peak, the slump of the late 1970s and even the stock market crash of 1987! Nevertheless, these models of 'Dynamic Stochastic General Equilibrium' are used to predict growth and as a basis for central banks to manipulate interest rates.[38] These models supposedly arm central bankers such that they can move quickly and easily to guide an economy to its target levels of growth, simply by varying the short-term interest rate. This might be nonsense, but it is dangerous nonsense.

> Much of the elegant theoretical structure that has been constructed in the last one hundred years in economics will be seen over the next decade to have provided a wrong focus and a misleading and ephemeral idea of what constitutes an equilibrium. If we consider two standard criteria for a scientific theory – prediction and explanation – economic theory has proved to say the least, inadequate. (Alan Kirman 1999)

The pursuit of some sort of equilibrium in economies is fool's gold. The long wave business cycles are an inbuilt feature of capitalism. This means that governments cannot smooth out the peaks and troughs, and indeed make them worse when they

---

36   Diggle, P. and Ormerod, P., *Be Bold for Growth* (London: Centre for Policy Studies, March 2010).

37   HM Treasury, *Trend Growth: New Evidence and Prospects* (London: HMSO, December 2006).

38   Known as the Taylor Rules, after the economist John Taylor's 1993 formulation, central bankers actually believe that interest rates should be governed by the prevailing (and likely) rate of inflation relative to its target, and the level of a country's economic output relative to its long-term trend.

attempt to do so. The reason this is so is that economies – and indeed societies – are complex systems that are difficult enough to fathom, let alone predict. Economic 'trends' – more exactly the patterns of trade and growth – are the outcome of numerous individual decisions by people and companies and, yes, by governments. In this Hayek and the Austrians are quite right.

Even so, econometricians will continue to pore over the minutiae of daily changing stock prices. They will tell you, on a daily basis, that the stock market 'gained on the back of' x, y or z, but they are unable to see historical trends or major events such as a credit crunch in the making.

> For a long while after the explosion of macroeconomics in the 1970s, the field looked like a battlefield. Over time however, largely because facts do not go away, a largely shared vision both of fluctuations and of methodology has emerged … The state of macro is good.[39]

This rosy assessment was published by the chief economist of the International Monetary Fund in August 2008, a few weeks before the collapse of Lehman Brothers. Whatever caused the 'Global Financial Crisis' and the recession, the IMF did not see it coming. Whatever the truth in all of this, and whether I am right to be so sceptical about government economic policy, depends to an extent on whether economics can be understood other than by reference to mathematical equations, equilibrium and plumbing.

---

39   Blanchard, O., *The State of Macro*, Cambridge, MA, MIT Working Paper, 2008.

Chapter 4
Real Economies, Real Places

Oh, London is a fine town,
A very famous city,
Where all the streets are paved with gold,
And all the maidens pretty.

George Colman the Younger, *The Heir at Law*, 1787

Economics is Natural

One of the delights of life is to visit a market, stroll amongst the stalls and stop to buy fresh fruit and veg, second-hand clothes, jams and honeys and handmade soap. If you stop to think about, the farmers and others who make and sell these things can do so because we wish to buy them at a price that suits us but also allows for the stall holders to make a profit. This is the secret to economic life. People produce and sell things to make a profit at a price we could not make the things for ourselves. This is no less true of iPods and mobile phones (good products according to the urban elites), or plasma televisions or cars (bad products). As long as there is free and fair competition, prices remain low and affordable. As competition increases, the cost of new products falls.

Of course, we also enjoy markets for their colour and life and the various levels of interaction that occur at them. Markets are a happy and enjoyable aspect of life, as natural as enjoying a family meal or watching other people perform. We love to buy and sell and trade and swap. This is the uncomplicated truth on which economics is based. At its simplest, economic life is a form of magic, even poetry. By this I mean not the machinations of macroeconomics, but rather the simple elegance of supply, demand and prices, or micro-economics as first conceptualised by Adam Smith. As we have seen, Smith was able to show that markets not only bring about the most efficient forms of production and consumption, they also result in the fairest distribution of goods and services. Generally speaking, when goods are produced in competitive free markets in which people trade at market prices, the allocation of these goods is fair and efficient.

Not everyone agrees that Smith was right about this. Those on the Left who only grudgingly accept market economics, concentrate not on capitalism's successes but on its alleged failures. In particular, instances of 'market failure' are put forward, such as 'externalities'. The usual example is where a producer or consumer does not meet the full costs of his consumption or production: the factory owner whose pricing does not include the costs of air pollution; or the car driver who likewise does not pay for her exhaust fumes. However, these 'externalities' can be internalised by paying levies for air quality, or indeed encouragement to install filtering systems. As for cars, we now pay a hefty mark-up in government taxes to pay for pollution and road construction and maintenance, while modern cars are fitted with catalytic convertors that render 95 per cent of exhaust emissions harmless. Producers and consumers alike respond to incentives and disincentives.

It is probably more accurate, then, to talk not of 'market failure' but markets that are missing.[1] The introduction of a market in air, for example, would reduce pollution, and indeed this is presumably the objective of cap-and-trade CO_2 schemes, misguided on anthropogenic global warming as they are.[2] Where markets are introduced, more efficient outcomes follow. It would be better for us all if there were markets for everything. However, this is not always possible at any given point in time, and so governments have a role to help shape new markets through laws and incentives. Smith himself saw the need to regulate markets to prevent collusion – this is why we have anti-trust laws – and to direct them to help deal with social matters. Hayek certainly accepts the need to deal with externalities and monopolies.

Take the story of Poland's re-emergence from the long winter of Soviet socialism, the first blooms of a new market economy. In the early 1990s, Poland invited economists from Harvard University to advise on the creation of a market economy. The approach recommended was radical, eschewing as it did the superstructure of 'financial architecture' and government regulation. Rather, the Polish government was advised to abolish price controls and overturn the ban on private enterprise. It did so on New Year's Eve 1991. Prices increased substantially and queues for everyday goods lengthened, the government only just managing to hold its nerve.

One spring day, the Minister for Finance was on his way to Parliament when he noticed a collection of tents and stalls in one of the city squares. On asking what this was, he was told it was a market. People from the countryside were selling fresh produce to city dwellers. It was economic to do so, because prices had risen to levels that made the effort of growing, transporting and running a stall worthwhile. Over the following weeks and months, as more producers joined the market, prices fell as competition took hold. Soon prices were reasonably low again, but this time there was also food to buy. This is what markets do.

Yet macroeconomics, whether Keynesian or Monetarist, Fisher or A. W. E. Phillips, has strayed further and further from this essential truth. The King's chancellors these days believe it is they who create wealth by 'economic management', by cutting interest rates and putting them up again, by increasing government spending and cutting it again. Their overall aim in all of this is to achieve 'stable prices' by balancing the level of unemployment against 'inflation'. This is a major error, leading to violent swings in economic policy, and one that

---

1   Landsburg, S., *The Armchair Economist* (New York: The Free Press, 1993).

2   Rightly the subject of another book. The author does not support the view that man-made emissions of carbon dioxide are the main cause of climate change.

fails completely to explain 'stagflation', a condition by which unemployment and inflation are both high. According to the theory, this is simply not possible. Real life, real economics is a grave disappointment.

In her last major work before her death,[3] Jane Jacobs argued that 'economic development is a version of natural development'. She argued that economies only succeed where there are economically creative and innovative people. Economic development is a non-linear system, argues Jacobs, such that economies make themselves up as they go along. She gives the example of the English language that continually adds new words and phrases but retains its overall meaning and role as a communication medium. Diverse economies expand in a rich environment, itself created by diverse use of local resources and imported materials, again as Smith argued. A 'gene pool' of work builds up over time, that is knowledge, skills, techniques and methods. This leads to a type of 'creative self-organisation' and a continual and continuing process of adaptation and improvisation. Development produces diversity but depends on co-development – that is to say trade – and because of this development is open-ended not pre-planned. Jacobs concludes that economic development – rather than *economics* – should be seen as a set of processes and principles we humans did not consciously invent and cannot transcend, but is rather part of the nature of human societies. Markets are characterised much more by disequilibrium than equilibrium.

In seeking an economic theory that more closely explains the complexity of markets, some economists have turned to the idea of open systems of the sort found in nature.

One such is Eric Beinhocker[4] who follows Jacobs in arguing that economics should be based on biological models as opposed to physics (Keynesianism) or plumbing (the Phillips curve). Beinhocker too argues that far too much attention has been focused on attempts to achieve 'balance' or equilibrium by weighing unemployment against inflation. He sees economies more as 'complex adaptive systems' like the Internet, the human brain or an ecosystem. Wealth, for Beinhocker, is created through an evolutionary process. He calls this 'complexity economics'.

Beinhocker's idea of evolutionary growth retains the notion of competition, and sees price signals as feedback loops sending important information about the ongoing dynamics of economies. Feedback loops can be both positive and negative, and crucially they are subject to time delays, so that economic policy-makers – even the smartest and best informed – are dealing with information that is already, to varying degrees, out-of-date. Beinhocker goes on to argue that since economies are non-linear, it is impossible to predict future events with certainty and that 'the only way to mitigate (business) cycles is to change the structure of the system itself'.[5] Human behaviour combined with the non-linear dynamics of open economic systems cannot but mean otherwise.

---

3   Jacobs, J., *The Nature of Economies* (New York: Vintage, 2000).

4   Beinhocker, E., *The Origin of Wealth* (London: Random House, 2007).

5   Ibid., p. 113.

Self-Generating Economies

According to the Second Law of Thermodynamics,[6] 'entropy', a measure of disorder or randomness in a system, is always increasing. There are two types of system: open and closed. In a closed system, there is no interaction with the external environment or any other system, so that neither energy nor information or matter can flow in or out. Since entropy is always increasing the system eventually comes to a rest – it dies. By contrast, in an open system, energy and matter flow in and out, thus reducing entropy. Open systems are dynamic and they change and adapt often, if not constantly. Sometimes they can be stable for a period of time, but more often they are complex and unpredictable. This may be tiresome for economic modellers, but it is good for the rest of us. For if systems or economies ever achieve a fixed state of equilibrium, the chances are they are dead. In order to maintain growth and levels of wealth creation, economic systems need regular infusions of energy.

According to Jane Jacobs, the crucially dynamic economic systems occur not at the national level, but rather in city regions. In dynamic cities and city regions, energy (or matter or information) comes from new work and imports from which further new work is in turn created (as imports are replaced to be produced locally). A portion of received energy must be devoted to capturing new energy, that is new imports. This 'self-fuelling'[7] is a process by which cities generate their own new work, and thus future rounds of creation and growth. So where does this new energy come from?

Jacobs had earlier proposed a model of city economic growth, which she refers to as 'The Two Reciprocating Systems of City Growth'.[8] Her argument is that cities achieve growth primarily through a process of exporting goods and services in order to earn surpluses with which to purchase imports. As the economy develops, more and more exports generate greater surpluses, during which time the division of labour amongst local producers becomes more complex. Various supply chains develop, so that networks of businesses provide inputs to the final export product. (An example in clothing might be the weaver, the button-maker, the stitcher, all supplying to a shirt exporting business.) Some of the producer service businesses might themselves become exporters in their own right. The outcome should be a dynamic network of local businesses, a good proportion of

---

6   The Second Law of Thermodynamics is also known as the Law of Increased Entropy. This holds that the quantity of matter/energy deteriorates gradually over time. Usable energy is inevitably used for productivity, growth and repair. In the process, usable energy is converted into unusable energy. Thus, usable energy is irretrievably lost in the form of unusable energy. 'Entropy' is a measure of unusable energy within a closed or isolated system. As usable energy decreases and unusable energy increases, 'entropy' increases. Entropy is thus a gauge of randomness or chaos within a closed system such that, as usable energy is irretrievably lost, disorganisation, randomness and chaos increase.

7   Jacobs, J., *The Nature of Economies* (New York: Vintage, 2000).

8   Jacobs, J., *The Economy of Cities* (London: Jonathan Cape, 1969).

which must export, others of which are producer input suppliers, and over time there will be a continual process of mergers, breakaways, new start-ups ... and failures too.

The next stage is very important, for over time a strong and/or growing city economy will develop the skills and the capacity to replace or substitute imports and make these products locally. Jacobs applies this model to the Japanese motorcycle industry in the 1920s, which grew from bicycle repair workshops that initially serviced and repaired imported English bicycles. It grew to include marques such as Honda, Suzuki and Yamaha. By this means, a city economy can then import other goods with its export surpluses and meanwhile the newly replaced imports may become another successful export product. Of course, during this time the city economy continues to export its existing goods and services, while the local division of labour becomes more diversified and complex. The wealth that is created is then re-invested in productive capacity, raw materials or stock; and a good proportion of this will also be spent by local citizens on consumer goods and services. The growth of local consumer spending in periods of rapid economic growth will closely be followed by, and in turn will create, increasing demand for new products – chocolates and coffee, fashions and jewels.

Jacobs goes on to demonstrate how these processes inter-lock and go on to produce multiplier effects for both exports (more local producers and exporters) and import-replacement (to meet local demand initially but later as new exports). She uses the examples of sixteenth-century London, Tokyo in the early twentieth century, and Chicago, to show that cities where these processes are self-generating and dynamic can enjoy periods of 'explosive growth'. Of course, they can also go into decline. Indeed, Jacobs notes that 'the processes have to be reinvented in cities which have become economically stagnant, for unless they are, nothing else can halt the city's decline'.[9] It is just this sort of approach that is having to be followed in cities such as Leipzig, whose economy had virtually died under Communism.[10]

This relationship of exporting, inter-trading, wealth creation and the development of local economies was present in Europe from about the tenth century onwards, but is particularly evident under early mercantile capitalism, industrial capitalism and late capitalism. Jacobs refers to this as a form of 'dynamic stability'. It is only found in dynamic cities and their regions. Dynamic stability depends on constant self-correction: bifurcations, positive and negative feedback loops and emergency adaptations. In market economies, prices are a form of feedback loop that automatically corrects maladjustments between supply and demand, as they did in Poland in 1992. However, these signals can be confused, not to say undermined, by things such as subsidies, tariffs, import taxes and by

---

9   Ibid., p. 198.

10   Gerkens, K., *Strategies and Tools for Shrinking Cities – the Example of Leipzig*, paper presented to the International Cities, Town Centres and Communities Conference, June 2005, Capricorn Coast, Queensland.

interest rate policies in so far as these manipulate currency values away from their market levels. As a general rule, tariffs should only be used to help establish baby industries, not to preserve traditional industries that are in decline. Emergency adaptations are items such as unemployment insurance, means of protecting bankrupt enterprises and individuals from creditors, safeguarding pensions and savings, welfare assistance, and charitable help in times of financial peril. These by their nature should be time-limited and removed or lessened as economic growth returns.

Real Places: Cities and Regions

What this means is that countries of themselves are not a single economy, but rather an aggregation of dynamic regions based around cities, bypassed places and laggard regions. Successful economic regions, based around dynamic cities, are places of complex variety where new work is added to old work to produce new products, processes and services. Such places, as we have seen, must export, but they also import and replace imports with new businesses, some of which in turn become exporters.

The important measurement of economic growth is not therefore aggregate levels of GDP across a country, but rather the economic health of key growth cities and their regions. Successful cities will be constantly producing new goods and services for export, but they will also be replacing imports with local production, providing new exports and also building up local consumption of personal goods and services. Thus, the key indicator of economic health is the ratio of total economic value to the value of imports.

Forgive me if all of this seems blindingly obvious and sensible; it is to normal people and especially business owners, but it is just too simple for economists to understand. They would rather fiddle about with interest rates and comment breathlessly on the up-to-the-minute movements in share prices. The latter are a form of feedback loop, and therefore important to understand, but not if one forgets how wealth creation occurs.

Some countries, such as Australia, are lucky enough to have large reserves of natural resources they can export, but they also contain economically moribund places where local GDP is stagnant or low, South Australia for example. Without the existence of dynamic economies elsewhere, the cities of China in our case, there would be no one to sell our resources to. In this way, economic development depends on co-development of other trading areas and centres. Without trade, there is no growth,[11] and without growth only stagnation and the decline of civilisation will follow. Only a handful of city regions achieve self-regenerating growth, building up networks of businesses and an ongoing capacity for innovation, places such as London or Milan or Singapore or Taiwan. The more successful

---

11   Montgomery, J., *The New Wealth of Cities* (Aldershot: Ashgate, 2007).

a city economy becomes, the more its geographical sphere of influence spreads over surrounding rural areas and settlements, such that these too become part of the growth pole. Regions that achieve this status enjoy economic prosperity and wealth creation. This is the secret to the success enjoyed by Milan, Barcelona, Turin, Stuttgart and Munich.

But there are other types of region, in fact Jacobs names four: supply regions, abandoned regions, cleared regions and transplant regions. Supply regions are largely agricultural areas whose main purpose is to supply food and primary produce to city regions – for example the old sugar cane fields of northern New South Wales or the great Steppes of the Ukraine. Their prosperity depends on being able to sell produce to city markets. Abandoned regions are places where jobs are in such short supply that people leave to seek opportunities elsewhere, for example South Wales in the UK, South Australia or Ireland for much of the twentieth century. Cleared regions are where well-meaning investments in technology lead to a collapse of employment on the land, so people must uproot and leave. This occurs these days in Africa and, to an extent, rural China and India. Transplant regions are places where governments offer incentives to big business to open branch plants in backward regions such as Scotland or the south of Italy – this almost never succeeds. Such regions remain a fiscal drag on productive city region economies unless they themselves become dynamic centres of enterprise and wealth creation. Dublin is managing this, as are Helsinki and Austin, Texas, but Edinburgh and Belfast are not.

One interesting question that this raises is how best to continue economic development through exporting and by import replacement and a further diversification of the division of labour. And here we come up against the role that currencies play in trade.

Why Currencies Matter

Currencies are units of exchange, that is the easy part to understand. They also achieve symbolic importance for societies, and people become attached to them. Ten years after the Euro was first introduced as a full-blown currency, many French, German and Dutch people still rue the passing of the Franc, Mark and Guilder. Denmark, Sweden and Norway have refused to part company with their respective kronas, Britain has retained the pound sterling. Denmark and Sweden are largely unaffected by the fiscal crisis of the Euro-states and have the option of currency devaluation. The point is that independent currencies, especially for small nations, play a centrally important role in economic development and wealth creation. Sadly, this role has been overlooked or is misunderstood in Euro-land and by those calling for more supranational currencies.

Wealth creation and economic development emerge through a process of trade whereby localised economies buy and sell from each other in increasingly complex and intricate ways. The barometer of how well an economy is doing was traditionally the valuation of its currency. If an economy was importing too much or not earning enough by exporting, the currency would shift in value to reflect this. This means that a well as being units of exchange, local currencies 'give valuable and corrective feedback on international trade'.[12] Currencies go down in value when an economy is faltering, and up in value when it is strong. If a currency falls, this is not only a signal that growth is slowing, it is also the means by which a correction is introduced, automatically, by the economic system itself. Devaluing currencies make exports cheaper and imports more expensive. This should help to stimulate international exports, and also make it more viable for local firms to replace imports by local production. By contrast, if an economy is strong its currency will increase and so its exports will earn more and imports will be cheaper. This is a version of Smith's 'invisible hand' applied to currencies and their role in economic development.

The trouble with supranational currencies is that they cannot possibly send these signals and automatically self-correct. In Europe, France and Germany have been locked into a cycle of low growth since the mid 1980s and setting up of the European Exchange Mechanism, an attempt to peg European currencies to each other. This ended badly for countries such as Britain, Italy and Portugal. By contrast, over the past 20 years smaller economies such as Ireland and Spain have grown more rapidly. The problem arises when central bankers attempt to set interest rates to balance growth against inflation. A rate that slows down Ireland has the effect of grinding the German economy to a halt; a rate that seeks to boost French economic development fans inflation in Spain. This means that at any point in time none of the economies of Europe is behaving as it would under its own currency. Repeat: none. Because of this none of these economies is receiving the signals that movements in currency values gives. None of them are self-correcting.

Think of it like this. Small national currencies are feedback loops and feedback controls, alerting us to changing patterns of trade and also automatically making adjustments. These feedback controls are built into the economic system itself, and so the corrections that are triggered are not discretionary but are precisely to the point: they correct the results of previous events and patterns of trade. It's a bit like the body's nerve system telling you that you are in pain, but simultaneously dispatching blood cells, endorphins and immune agents to correct the problem.

Larger countries with a single currency covering a large geographical expanse may also struggle to self-correct. This is because currencies like the US and Australian dollars apply over a range of local and regional economies. These include dynamic growth poles, but also laggard regions and bypassed places.

In the UK, London is a dynamic economy, but Scotland is a laggard region. In the United States, dynamic areas of wealth creation are found in Silicon Valley, Seattle, Austin, Boston, San Diego, eastern Pennsylvania and LA to some extent. Complexes of dynamic wealth creation are organised by and large around cities and their regions: London, Milan, Boston, LA, Barcelona, Stuttgart, Berlin,

---

12   Jacobs, J., *The Nature of Economies* (New York: Vintage, 2000), p. 112.

Dublin, Copenhagen, Seattle, São Paulo, Tokyo, Osaka, Shanghai, Shenzhen, Seoul, Helsinki and so on. Other places get along OK, but there are several economic black holes such as Detroit, Pittsburgh, the Appalachians and these days San Francisco. Once great city economies such as Pittsburgh did not realise until too late that their pattern of trade was in serious decline – they missed the signals and there was no automatic self-correction. Instead of diversifying its economy, Pittsburgh died. In Australia, the best example of a laggard region with a stagnant economy is Adelaide.

It should come as no surprise, therefore, that the most successful economies in recent times have been small countries with their own currencies, places like Denmark and Norway or the Baltic states of Latvia and Estonia, or especially Hong Kong, Taiwan and Singapore. As sovereign city states, Singapore and Hong Kong (despite Chinese rule) have currencies that reflect their own trade situation.

As in much of macroeconomics, advocates of large supranational currencies take the real business of everyday buying and selling for granted. They prefer to fiddle about with 'the architecture', ignoring how real economic development works, its many variations and complexity. They force it into a set of straitjackets, most damagingly constructs like the Euro. We should be thankful that no one is calling for a world currency and world government. They're not, are they?

Transactions of Decline

Many advanced economies are replete with formerly dynamic city and city region economies that became laggards: Glasgow, Belfast, Liverpool, Detroit, Chicago, Pittsburgh, Brooklyn … all of these places failed to diversify their economies, partly at least because they failed to receive the signals and self-correction that local currencies would have produced. They all failed to act in time as trade in their staple industries declined. Economies that lose export work without compensating for these losses are doomed to decline. They suffer in the end for a lack of economic discipline that local currencies bring to bear. They become locked into 'transactions of decline'.[13]

During the 1960s, for example, the Labour government of the United Kingdom was keen to see economic activity grow in Scotland where the old industries of steel-making, heavy engineering and shipbuilding were already in decline. Economic planners decided to offer tax incentives and grants to companies who would open factories in Scotland. One such was the Rootes Motor Company that, famously, produced the Hillman Imp at its Linwood factory near Glasgow. The venture was a failure from the start: the cars were not well built, the workforce unreliable, many days were lost in industrial disputes and the presence of the factory did comparatively little to build networks of suppliers, most parts being trucked in from factories in the West Midlands. In seeking to maintain political

---

13   Jacobs, J., *The Economy of Cities* (London: Jonathon Cape, 1969).

support in Scotland, the government was not helping to recreate a dynamic economy. Indeed it undermined the formation of such an economy, because its actions helped to blunt innovation and economic self-development. In turn, this leads to a decline in new work, exporting and import replacement. This is what is meant by 'transactions of decline'.

It gets worse. Welfare programmes, nationally set wage rates across industries, grants and subsidies, government spending on military contracts – all of these further undermine the capacity of a city region to improvise and grow new work. These are all forms of 'subsidy transactions'. Their effect is to drive out market transactions over time. An economy that does not innovate cannot replace imports and thus create new work. Were this not the case, then regions that are stagnant would achieve great wealth simply by spending government money, or to put it another way by managing and increasing levels of demand (as Marx and Keynes supposed). Meanwhile, of course, any profits made by transplant factories tend to be 'repatriated' to head office and shareholders, so that only a proportion of new wealth is retained in the city or region.

Over time, the proportion of the city-region's wealth (or GDP) that is made up of exports will stagnate and may decline; but certainly the amount of innovative new work that comes from import replacement falls as a proportion of total work. The rate of firm formation is sluggish and there is often barely enough work for established businesses. Opportunities for business development or even employment in growing sectors are restricted, and so the young and well-qualified leave for more dynamic city economies.

Mindful of the need to be seen to be doing something, central governments tend to respond by offering more subsidies, more transplants and more government contracts. Rather than bringing about an economic renaissance, this produces further relative and often real decline. Resources dedicated to social services increase as a proportion of total economic activity, and so too does the number of state and other public sector employees. Unless these are paid for by central government, the drain on local and state government resources increases, and running enterprises can become even harder. If not enough new work and new wealth is created, the market for local services such as restaurants and personal services is more or less fixed. Some cities, rather than company towns, become government towns. As time goes on these lose more and more energy and stagnate economically. The only way out of the cycle of stagnation and decline is to regenerate a dynamic self-correcting economy.

Clusters, Networks and Creative Milieu

There is a large literature in economic geography that seeks to explain why growth occurs in cities and city regions. Michael Porter, for example, in his book *The*

Competitive Advantage of Nations,[14] argues that competitive success tends to concentrate in particular industries and groups of inter-connected industries. For Porter, the determinants of competitive advantage are four-fold: business strategy, structure and rivalry so as to encourage innovation, investment and competition; 'factor conditions', notably the presence of specialist skills, technology and infrastructure; related and supporting industries who supply specialist services and imports, and access to technology and innovation; and 'demand conditions' in the form of sophisticated and demanding customers. Porter argues that successful industries tend to co-locate in dynamic clusters. A 'cluster' is a grouping of industries linked together through customer, supplier and other relationships which enhance competitive advantage. These clusters are characterised by the presence of internationally competitive firms, which also continuously upgrade and innovate.

This argument is broadly consistent with the economic literature on industrial districts and the work on 'agglomeration' by Alfred Marshall,[15] dating from the late nineteenth century. Marshall argued that there were competitive advantages to firms who 'agglomerate', because of access to available skilled labour, shared technologies and inter-trading between firms (a form of Smith's division of labour). This happens at key locations within cities, but also – for certain activities – across wider city regions as mobility improves. It is these places – districts, cities and city regions – that are the engines of economic development.

Richard Florida[16] and Charles Landry[17] have, separately, set out the conditions that underpin the emergence of 'creative cities'. This includes, in Landry's conception, such matters as competition for patents, a high skills base, chance meetings and collaborations and people gravitating to the right cities at certain points in time. For Florida, as well as technological competence, the most important feature of a city's creative economy is the wider sense of 'tolerance' for artists, their lifestyles and for new work and genres. In this, Florida is very close to Hippolyte Taine's[18] concept of the 'creative milieu'.

Taine argues that where creative milieux exist, these tend to be underpinned by 'a general state of manners and mind', producing in turn a 'moral temperature' which allows talent and artistic creativity to develop in particular places at particular times.[19] Taine asserts that artists and creative innovators always exist within human societies, and so the question becomes one of whether they are allowed or encouraged to pursue their art. Moreover, such people tend only to innovate,

---

14   Porter, M., *The Competitive Advantage of Nations* (London: Collier Macmillan, 1990).

15   Marshall, A., *Principles of Economics* (London: Macmillan, 1920).

16   Florida, R., *The Rise of the Creative Class: And How it's Transforming Work, Leisure, Community and Everyday Life* (New York: Perseus, 2002).

17   Landry, C., *The Creative City* (London: Earthscan, 2000).

18   Hall, P. *Cities in Civilisation* (London: Weidenfeld and Nicolson, 1998).

19   Taine, H., *Philosephie de l'Art*, 1865, as translated by Peter Hall, ibid., pp. 15–16.

at least in their early years, where they have access to stimuli, opportunities to meet other people and freedom from censorship and heavy-handed regulation. This suggests that not only is creative genius itself essential to progress, but so too are the economic, cultural, moral and even built environments in which artists and inventors live. This may well provide the clue to why certain cities are or have been creative milieu, and others probably never will be.

Conceptions of such 'creative milieux' were developed in the modern literature by the Swedish urban historians Gunnar Törnqvist and Ake Andersson over 25 years ago. Törnqvist developed his own concept of the creative milieu in 1978, arguing that there were four key features:[20] information (which must be exchanged and inter-traded); knowledge (bodies of work and data-bases); competence in certain activities; and creativity, which combines the other three features to create new products, ideas and processes. In this way, creative places have a set of characteristics that, in most cases, take a long time to evolve and develop. It takes time to build up libraries, archives, data-bases and traditional skills. Such places come to have a recognised set of creative specialisms, and these in turn act as a magnet to attract further generations of creative people. This is what happens in London and New York, but also Milan and Helsinki. Artists, in particular, are attracted to places with a diversity of trades and businesses, and a strong element of chaos and the chance encounter.

Let's take an example. The acknowledged father of the Scottish Enlightenment was Henry Home, born in 1696. Home would later take the title Lord Kames as a judge at the Court of Sessions. He became a member of the Scottish bar and was friends with the poet Allan Ramsey (1685–1758). From 1757, Home became curator of the Advocates' Library which, with the help of Thomas Ruddimen, he built into one of the most extensive libraries in Britain, covering not only law but also philosophy, history and geography, anthropology and sociology. This library would provide the store of knowledge that gave rise to the Edinburgh Enlightenment.

Home embarked upon his quest to understand the nature of man. Fitting his reading and writing in between his duties as an advocate, he enjoyed the arts and discussions with fellow intellectuals in the evenings – the beginnings of a tradition that would last 100 years. Regular attendees included John Millar, who would later become the University of Glasgow's first Professor of Civil Law, the young Adam Smith and James Boswell (advocate, writer and later biographer of Dr Johnson), and David Hume who was, in fact, a distant relative. Home's own publications include *Essays on the Principles of Morality and Natural Religion* (1751) and *Historical Law Tracts* (1758). Home would conclude that the happiest societies can be found where the law, culture and 'manners' match.

By the 1760s Edinburgh's reputation as a centre of intellectual and artistic life was matched only by London and Paris. Those attracted to Edinburgh

---

20   Törnqvist, G., 'Creativity and the Renewal of Regional Life', in Buttimer, A. (ed.), *Creativity and Context* (Lund: Gleerup, 1983).

included thinkers, scholars and artists such as Robert Adam, Benjamin Franklin, Robert Burns, Allan Ramsey the portrait artist, William Robertson and Adam Ferguson. Numerous clubs and societies were set up, including the Oyster Club, the Miner Club, the Select Society and the Edinburgh Society for Encouraging Arts, Sciences, Manufacture and Agriculture in Scotland, founded in 1762. Many of these clubs met in taverns. The most important works to emerge from this period would be Hume's *Political Discourses* (1752), Smith's *Theory of Moral Sentiments* (1759) and *The Wealth of Nations* (1776) and Adam Ferguson's *Essay on the History of Civil Society* (1767). These ideas would resonate far beyond the borders of Scotland, to England certainly, but also to Germany, across Europe and onto America, where many of them would be enshrined in the constitution, the rule of law, the market economy and concepts of civilisation. For a while at least, Edinburgh was a creative milieu, although it never became a self-generating city region economy as its rival Glasgow did from the mid eighteenth to the mid twentieth century.

Ake Andersson[21] argues that creative milieux are cities which have developed almost subliminal abilities to produce new work in art, technology and science. Such places tend to be culturally diverse (in terms of tastes and preferences, rather necessarily than ethnic variety), rich in knowledge, have a store of skills and competencies, and are well-connected through communications infrastructure. For Andersson, creative milieux are predicated on six essential conditions. The first of these is a sound financial base, so that capital is available to develop new products and services, but regulation and taxation must be light. This side of the equation is often overlooked by those that assume that all it takes to be successful is a few art galleries. There must, as a prerequisite, be an existing base of original knowledge and competence, but incentives to encourage experimentation and the exploration and exploitation of new opportunities will also be necessary. Good communications and infrastructure are important to transport goods and services to export markets, but also to enable inter-trading and the development of myriad producer service relationships. Uncertainty over the future direction of scientific and technological progress is also helpful, paradoxically, as this encourages trial and error. Finally, creative people welcome the stimulus of the arts, entertainment and even opportunities to transgress.

These latter attributes, especially, suggest that it is quite likely that creative milieux, particularly in the artistic fields, will tend to agglomerate around places – usually cities – which are themselves interesting in terms of their cultural life, entertainment, street life, urban form and architecture. This means that creative milieux are comprised of clusters of industries, networks of firms and individuals, social relations and cultural life; and that they tend to occur in geographical space, that is to say cities and city regions. Successful creative milieux tend thus also to be self-generating urban and city-regional economies.

---

21   Andersson, A., 'Creativity and Regional Development', *Papers of the Regional Science Association*, 56, 1985.

Commentary

In this chapter, I have argued that economic development (not *economics*) should be seen as a non-linear system because economies make themselves up as they go along. They do so in cities, city regions and resource regions, so that a national economy is simply the aggregate of such places and laggard regions. Diverse city and city-regional economies expand in a rich environment, itself created by diverse use of local resources and imported materials. A tradition of work builds up over time, that is knowledge, skills, techniques and methods. This leads to a type of self-propelling business network and a continual and continuing process of adaptation and improvisation, including in the arts and civil life. All cities must at some point achieve this dynamic, otherwise they would not have become cities. Cities and city regions are open systems because they trade with other places. Trade creates wealth. And so, dynamic economies are based in real places, that is to say growing cities and regions; they are not just an aggregate of GDP across a nation.

Some implications flow from this. For one thing, it is the private sector that creates wealth, not governments. So business owners and people setting up in business know best what is good for their business, livelihood and the place and sector of which they are part, not macroeconomists. Moreover, because successful economies are open-ended rather than goal-oriented, setting targets or 'picking winners' is a waste of time. Economic growth and wealth creation depend on a process of continual innovation and improvisation, a set of conditions to which government is not suited. Because of this, governments who believe in 'firm, clear decision-making' and 'resolute purpose' will usually fail. The lesson is that economic life cannot be planned; it can only be helped – or hindered.

The other sad truth is that once dynamic city-region economies can stagnate and die. The cradle of the industrial revolution was Birmingham[22] with all its wonderfully inventive new entrepreneurs in the mid eighteenth century. It was in Birmingham that steam was first harnessed to industrial production, that the world's first iron bridge was built and that the great pottery industry of the Midlands would grow. This came about because of the inventiveness of people such as Erasmus Darwin and James Watt, Josiah Wedgwood, the preacher and chemist Joseph Priestley and the great entrepreneur Matthew Boulton and his 'manufactory' at Soho. Others involved at the time included the Scots chemist James Kier and the clock maker John Whitehurst. Known as the Lunar Society of Birmingham, because they met monthly on the Monday night nearest to the full moon (so they could ride home by the light of the moon), these were the amateur experimenters, inventors and entrepreneurs that shaped the modern world.[23] Many of them were either Scottish or had studied in Edinburgh and Glasgow in the preceding years.

---

22   Jacobs, J. *The Economy of Cities* (London: Jonathan Cape, 1969).

23   Unglow, J., *The Lunar Men: The Friends Who Made the Future* (London: Faber & Faber, 2002).

Between them they would alter the course of geology and chemistry, experiment with electricity, develop the bone china and glass industries, build canals, develop steam power, experiment in mechanical engineering, develop the science of botany and even the important activity of road building.

Throughout the nineteenth century and into the twentieth century Birmingham and the West Midlands was a great centre of innovation and adaptation, especially in light engineering. This was also the home of the British car industry that grew impressively in the 1930s, 1950s and 1960s, but became moribund in the 1970s. Marques such as MG, Jaguar, Aston Martin, Alvis, Sunbeam, Rover, Triumph, Austin – all developed in the Midlands, and Morris not far away in Oxford. Most are now no more. The West Midlands was once a strong, dynamic, self-generating economy – an economic cluster – but it sadly experienced serious economic decline. The question is why? Perhaps some more examples will shed light on why city economies grow and decline.

Chapter 5
Growth and Decline:
Part I – Merchants and Mercantile Capitalism

What is a city? A city is its people. A city is alive ... (It) can afford to sustain every kind of craftsman and make him a specialist for a lifetime ... The specialists are gone, their work has been destroyed ... the goldsmith, the coppersmith, the weaver, the potter – their work has been destroyed. The woven fabric has decayed, the bronze has perished, the gold has been stolen. All that remains is the work of the masons.

Joseph Bronowski, *The Ascent of Man*, 1973

Bronowski, in the above quote, was referring to the collapse of the Greek city state. His argument was that specialist forms of work gave rise to the city and remained its life-blood. Cities are the places where work is organised around specialisms, exchange, consumption, trade and innovation. It was this realisation that prompted Adam Smith to write *The Wealth of Nations*, fascinated as he was by the prosperity of Kirkcaldy and the growth of Glasgow during the mid-eighteenth century.[1]

From early times cities have grown, and prospered with the development of trade. Once important trading centres have also declined. This growth, of course, developed on the back of previous waves or episodes of growth, themselves fuelled by trade. The historian Henri Pirenne charts the development of trade in Northern and Western Europe in the tenth century,[2] arguing that trading centres took a long time to develop as they grew from crossroad camps, fords and small ports. Trade, initially in grains, livestock, fish, salt, wool and furs, developed as people learned craft skills in cloth or leather goods or in pots and pans for cooking. Local consumer trades developed such as innkeeping and running brothels, while the all-important activity of shipbuilding and wagon-making developed. In this way, the early trading centres became centres of craft manufacturing. And by specialising in particular crafts and craft goods, the emerging cities were able to expand trade in volume, value and geographically. From this developed the medieval guilds, associations of craftsmen some of whom were also merchants. Production for export would thus expand as new markets opened up, and this in turn would feed more rounds of growth despite the vicissitudes of plague, war, great fires and natural disasters. From these small beginnings, ports and market towns would emerge, some of them such as London, Paris and Hamburg becoming great cities.

---

1 Phillipson, N., *Adam Smith: An Enlightened Life* (London: Allen Lane, 2010).

2 Pirenne, H. *Medieval Cities: Their Origins and the Revival of Trade*, translated by F. D. Halsey (Princeton: Princeton University Press, 1969).

This process built upon itself over the course of several centuries. But economic development is never a smooth, linear progression, and so the trading posts that became craft production centres, that became export centres for manufactured goods, that became small cities, grew in episodes of expansion punctuated by periods of stagnation and in some cases collapse. So although the long waves, as conceptualised by Kondratieff himself, refer only to industrial capitalism, a similar pattern of growth punctuated by periodic downturns is observable over a much longer period of time. I intend to show this in the examples that follow: the Scottish burghs of the sixteenth and seventeenth centuries, Amsterdam, the Hanseatic League and even the great cities of the Chinese Eastern Seaboard. We begin with the Italian city states that flourished from the tenth to the fifteenth century.

Italian City States: Venice and Florence

Venice in the thirteenth century opened up trade to the East, becoming a great trading and artistic centre in the process, and also a beautiful city. Venice grew from the sixth century as its founders – refugees from Padua – sought refuge from the plunder and anarchy of the Dark Ages. Because of its location on salt marshes and mud flats it was able to trade in salt with older cities such as Constantinople. It also exported timber for shipbuilding. As trade grew, Venice became a depot, a point of exchange for cargoes, mainly resource goods and raw materials moving East and West. From the tenth and eleventh centuries Venice 'had become an explosively growing city with an expanding market for raw materials from the west and North of Europe'.[3] The city began to produce craft goods of its own, using materials imported from other small cities, such as leather, cloth, copper, furs, amber and iron. Slowly at first, but gathering steam by the tenth century, Venice grew to become the major trading and manufacturing city of the age, as trade increased with cities such as London, Antwerp and Cordoba.[4] This process was well established by the time the Polos made their voyage to China.

With the wealth created from trade and craft production, Venice was able to build a beautiful city from as early as the twelfth century – the old Campanile was built in 1180, and the Ducal Palace in 1300.[5] The Piazza San Marco was a functioning city space by 976, and by the sixteenth century an important market place. Meanwhile the shipbuilding industry grew at the Arsenal, and the glass industry (on the island of Muran) during the thirteenth century. Culturally, Venice made great breakthroughs in architecture and design, but also in theatre (Commedia

---

3   Jacobs, J., *The Economy of Cities* (New York: Vintage Books, 1969), pp. 173–4.

4   Girouard, M., *Cities and People* (New Haven: Yale University Press, 1985). See Chapter 5, 'Bruges and Venice'.

5   Mumford, L., *The City in History* (New York: Harvest, 1961).

del Arte) and music (Monteverdi's Vespers). The Venice we see today was built on trade, without which there would have been nothing for Canaletto to paint.

A century or two later, Florence developed a flourishing economy based on the woollen industry initially, and later banking and commerce,[6] and this in turn led to a period of growth, city-building and artistic development – the Renaissance. At the beginning of the fifteenth century – the *quattrocento* – Florence had suffered two outbreaks of plague within 50 years, and its economy had stagnated. This brought commerce to a halt, following as it did a period of heavy taxation to fund a drawn-out war with the Viscontis of Milan. A series of earlier banking collapses in the 1340s had already weakened the economy, while the Black Death of 1348 had previously cut the population from 80,000 to 30,000. The likelihood of a Renaissance would not have seemed strong at a time of severe economic decline, the plague, a growth in poverty and falling land prices.

Even so, Florence remained a wealthier and more advanced city than most. This is because the wealth creation that helped spark the Renaissance occurred not contemporaneously but up to 50 years earlier. According to Robert Lopez[7] nothing less than the birth of capitalism occurred not in the *quattrocento* but in the *trecento* (the fourteenth century). For at this time a steady accumulation of capital (money and goods) was accompanied by complex patterns of trade, the use of credit, complicated bookkeeping, a growing division of labour and increased competition. This extended to the development of 'modern' banking by merchant families such as the Bardi, Peruzzi and the Medici. The bulk of trade in the *trecento* was not in the fine arts at all, but rather in the crafts and, most importantly, the wool industry and export of finished cloth.[8] By the mid-fifteenth century Florence was perhaps the largest textile-manufacturing city in Europe, predominantly in wool but also silk. By this time the Medici had companies in many other European cities, notably Geneva, London, Milan, Pisa, Avignon and Rome.

The Renaissance of 1400–1430 was built on wealth, wealth that had been accumulated over 50 years earlier. The key figures in the Renaissance were of course the artists, initially all craftsmen who had learned their trades in the guilds and workshops. Gitto, Brunelleschi and Leonardo were painters and sculptors, but also architects. Brunelleschi began as a goldsmith. Pisarello and Verrochio were also goldsmiths who became sculptors and painters. Raphael was a painter and architect, as was Michelangelo who was also, of course, a sculptor. Ghiberti was also a goldsmith who became a bronze-caster and sculptor; Donatello, his pupil, likewise. Because the artists themselves had served apprenticeships in the guilds and workshops, they had developed highly accomplished skills, so that they would

---

6   Roover de, R., *The Rise and Decline of the Medici Bank* (Cambridge, MA: Harvard University Press, 1963).

7   Lopez, R. S., 'The Trade of Medieval Europe', in Postan, M. and Rich E. E. (eds), *The Cambridge Economic History of Europe, 2: Trade and Industry in the Middle Ages* (Cambridge: Cambridge University Press, 1952), pp. 257–354.

8   Brucker, G., *Renaissance Florence* (Berkeley: University of California Press, 1983).

emerge as a recognisable 'class' at the same time that a market for decorative arts and architecture came into being. In a little over 30 years, they would change completely the history of art and architecture.

A further explanation for the Renaissance is suggested by Paul Robert Walker, who argues that a series of design competitions sparked a feud between Brunelleschi and Ghiberti, and it was this tension which sparked the Renaissance. Walker charts the story of the competition to design the doors for the north side of the Baptistry (the church of John the Baptist), a competition in the end that Ghiberti was to win in 1401. Having lost the commission, Brunelleschi left Florence for Rome, accompanied by Donatello. The two men would undertake an astonishing survey of Rome, making drawings of a great many buildings, measuring street and block widths, examining the foundations of ancient monuments and estimating building heights.[9] Although the Dome of Santa Maria del Fiore is Brunelleschi's most famous work, an even greater contribution was the rediscovery of perspective in drawing and painting, taken up notably by Masaccio, as without this there would have been no Renaissance.

Brunelleschi went on to secure many private commissions to design buildings and make sculptures for the city fathers (the *Signoria*), wealthy bankers and merchants and the Church. In the meantime, slowly at first but with increasing regularity, other artists were commissioned to execute public sculptures in the city. Of prime importance were Donatello's sculptures of David and St John the Evangelist, and the commissioning of statuary for the Orsanmichele church. Over a period of several years important works were commissioned from Brunelleschi, Donatello, Nanni and Ghiberti. These would form the centrepiece of a larger programme of public religious art. Sparked by these public commissions – both by the *Signoria* and the Church – the sheer amount of sculptures and paintings produced would later owe much to individual patronage, especially by the wealthy bankers and merchants. By the 1450s, Florence was enjoying an economic boom and at least part of this was spent on art and city building.

The conditions for the Renaissance were laid by the creation of wealth in the *trecento*, largely by the wool industry and trade. The creative 'spark' for the Renaissance occurred in the early 1400s, and this involved not only the application of highly developed craft skills, but also the rediscovery of classical architecture and perspective. The individuals of the day – Brunelleschi, Ghiberti and Donatello – were of key significance. But so too were the Church and city state who commissioned new sculpture, decorative door panels and buildings. Eventually the taste for art would be taken up more widely, certainly by the merchants but also the middle classes, so that demand for art of itself would increase during a period of economic prosperity. To put it another way, the underpinning of the Renaissance was the wealth generated during a previous wave of prosperity, the 'factor conditions' were the workshop system and the artists themselves, the

9   See Manetti, A., *The Life of Brunelleschi*, edited by Howard Saalman and translated by Catherine Enggass (Philadelphia: Pennsylvania State University Press, 1970).

enabling device was public patronage and the eventual boom was occasioned by a new cycle of wealth creators and demand for art. This broad pattern can be seen in any city that has become a major artistic centre.

The Scottish Burghs

By the fourteenth century Kirkcaldy was already a town of some consequence, having burgh status and therefore the right to trade freely in Scotland and overseas. By the early sixteenth century there was a small harbour and the town was developing as a centre of regional trade. Goods were imported from England, Ireland and the Low Countries in exchange for locally produced coarse cloth, nails and salt, as well as raw materials such as hides, wool, herring, salmon, coal and timber. A century later its merchants had extended their reach to France and the Baltic. By 1644 Kirkcaldy was trading with the Baltic and France, the town had a population of around 4,500, a fleet of around 100 ships, a complex guild system and a town council. By 1688, the town's tax returns reveal that it had become the sixth or seventh most important burgh in Scotland. This was a direct result of the growth of the linen industry, which would help transform the economy of eastern Scotland.[10]

By the 1730s, Kirkcaldy had turned itself into an effective entrepreneurial port, importing flax from Holland, Riga and St Petersburg for a local spinning and weaving industry. Skilled flax workers and weavers were recruited from abroad and a stamp-master system was introduced to guarantee the quality of local cloth. By the 1740s Kirkcaldy was exporting checks and tickings and napkins to England and the colonies. An annual market for linen cloth was established on the first Wednesday of July to encourage the local linen trade. In 1733, the town was producing 177,740 yards of stamped linen per year for England and the home market; by 1743 production had nearly doubled, and by 1790 output was running at about 900,000 yards, worth around £45,000.[11]

There then followed a period of further economic activity in Kirkcaldy: stocking manufacturing began in 1773, cotton manufacturing in the 1780s and shipbuilding in 1788. The town's population grew rapidly so that by the early eighteenth century Kirkcaldy was a small but prosperous town with a developed system of commerce.

This was a story repeated across several Scottish burghs during the eighteenth century as trade expanded with England, the Baltic and then America. Borrowstounness or Bo'ness is only 30 miles from Kirkcaldy, on the southern side of the Forth Estuary. A settlement from Roman times, by the seventeenth

---

10   Smith, R., Lawson, A. and Hume, J. R., *The Making of Scotland: A Comprehensive Guide to the Growth of its Cities, Towns, and Villages* (Edinburgh: Canongate, 2002).

11   Phillipson, N., *Adam Smith: An Enlightened Life* (London: Allen Lane, 2010), Chapter 1.

century the town was a centre for salt production and whaling, and it also imported timber from Scandinavia.[12] By the mid-eighteenth century it had a coal industry at Kinneil, and indeed it was here that James Watt developed his steam engine, originally intended to power water pumps in coal mines. The town's economy was linked with Edinburgh, which provided an important market for its salt and coal.[13] The local economy diversified into pottery during the nineteenth century, but the town lost out to west coast ports in the trade with America. By the late nineteenth century its importance as a port had been taken over by Grangemouth, a few miles further up the Forth.

Adam Smith grew up in Kirkcaldy, and was able to study its economy first-hand. He also came to know Glasgow well as a student of Glasgow University from 1737 to 1740, and later as Professor of Moral Philosophy, 1751–1763. During the sixteenth century most of Glasgow's mercantile trade had been confined to coastal trade in the west of Scotland, but in the early seventeenth century, business began to expand. At this time, merchants were trading wine and salt with France, luxury goods and foodstuffs with Holland, and timber with Norway. In exchange, Glasgow and its west coast hinterland exported linens and yarn down the west coast of England and even to London. By the late seventeenth century Glasgow was trading with the Canaries, the Azores and Madeira, with the English colonies in the Caribbean and with their plantations in the Carolinas, Virginia, New Jersey, New York and Massachusetts. There was also an expansion in trade with Norway and the Baltic. This was mainly in primary commodities such as cattle, hides, leather, herring and coal; and for luxury goods such as wines, brandies and fine textiles and raw materials like sugar, flax and hemp.

But it was the tobacco trade that became the source of the city's enormous wealth in the middle decades of the eighteenth century. Glasgow was ideally placed on the west coast of Scotland – on the River Clyde – for a shipping trade with Virginia and Carolina.

During a visit in 1724, Daniel Defoe observed:

> Glasgow is indeed, a very fine City: the four principal Streets are the fairest for Breadth, and the finest built that I have ever seen in one City together. The Houses are all of Stone, and generally equal and uniform in Height, as well as in Front; the lower story generally stands on vast Square Dorick Columns, not round Pillars, and Arches between give Passage into the Shops, adding to the Strength as well as Beauty of the Building; in a Word, 'tis the cleanest and beautifullest, and best built City in Britain, London excepted.[14]

---

12   Salmon, T. J., *Borrowstounness and district, being historical sketches of Kinneil, Carriden, and Bo'ness, c. 1550-1850* (Edinburgh: Scot W. Hodge, 1913).

13   Lynch, M., *The Early Modern Town in Scotland* (North Ryde: Croom Helm, 1987).

14   Phillipson, N., *Adam Smith: An Enlightened Life* (London: Allen Lane, 2010), Chapter 2.

By Smith's day, Glasgow was importing and re-exporting more than London and the English outports combined, and it was becoming one of the most important entrepôts in trade between the Americas and the Caribbean, and France, north Germany, the Baltic and Russia. Glasgow was shipping and warehousing tobacco and sugar as well as coffee, cheese, ginger, rum, canes, cottons, tar, canvas and gunpowder bound for Europe in exchange for European goods bound for America. This set the foundation for a period of pronounced wealth creation and city building. Tobacco merchants, with their trading links and capital resources, were going into businesses such as sugar refining, rope manufacture, iron works, tanneries and the leather business, bottle-making, and the manufacture of stockings and hats. There was also brewing, tanning, dyeing, chemical works and print works and ribbon-making. Later, these same merchants would branch out into iron and steel production, notably at the famous Carron ironworks near Falkirk, and shipbuilding.

Craft trades flourished along with a rising demand for coaches and sedan chairs, exotic and expensive foods and fashions. By 1751, the city's economy was supporting new newspapers, taverns, coffee-houses, public entertainments, shows and exhibitions of works of art. This was symptomatic of the general expansion of mercantile wealth across Europe at that time, notably in London and Amsterdam. Between 1750 and 1775 new public arcades and piazzas were being erected in the city centre and 12 new streets and squares were being developed to cater for a growing population and the increasingly sophisticated tastes of the tobacco lords.

Glasgow then, in a period of only 100 years or so, had grown from a small trading port serving the small towns of western central Scotland to a major trading and manufacturing centre; it expanded particularly with the growth of trade across the Atlantic, with the new world colonies. However, with the American Revolution of 1775, the Atlantic trade declined dramatically at a time when economic growth more generally was slowing. As Peter Hall puts it, 'Glasgow had to find another source of livelihood'.[15] It was able to do so because of wealth already accumulated, the development (in Edinburgh) of a Scottish banking system and technological developments in steam power and engines. The city was, it seems by accident, ideally placed to become the world's leading shipbuilding centre during and following the industrial revolution, continuing production until the early 1970s. In this way, Glasgow enjoyed not one but two golden ages of rapid wealth creation: in the eighteenth century based on mercantile trade and the tobacco industry; and in the nineteenth century based on steam and shipbuilding. This carried on into the early twentieth century, but by the 1960s Glasgow's great days as an economic pioneer were over.

---

15   Hall, P., *Cities in Civilisation* (London: Weidenfeld and Nicolson, 1998), Chapter 11.

The Hanseatic League

The Hanseatic League was initially formed in the thirteenth century as a loose trading block, not of countries as say in the case of the EU today, but of city-based guilds and merchants.[16] It lasted until the seventeenth century. It is rumoured to have begun in the north German town of Lubeck which was to become a great centre of sea-borne trade, situated as it was strategically between the North Sea and the Baltic Sea, but also along the 'Salt Road', that was Hamburg to Lubeck. The salt in question was mined at Kiel. The word 'Hanse' came to represent membership of a trade organisation run by city merchant guilds. The Hanseatic League was formally created in 1358, although by this time the trade routes and many partner cities had been long established.

Hansa societies secured trading privileges for their members, notably in access to markets and in the granting of royal seals. The League also protected ships from piracy, trained pilots and built lighthouses. Alliances were formed between cities such as Lubeck, Hamburg and Cologne, in Scania and even London (now the site of Cannon Street Station). Over time, trade expanded eastwards across the Baltic Sea as far as Helsinki and Novgorod in Russia. During the period of its ascendancy, membership of the Hanseatic League fluctuated from 70 to 170 cities.[17] Members included Bruges, Bergen, Boston, King's Lynn, Hull, Ipswich and York, Gdansk, Tallinn and Riga, Stockholm, Dortmund, Hamburg, Bremen, Newcastle, Edinburgh and Aberdeen. All of the cities of the Hanseatic League occupied strategic positions along the sea trade routes.

Trade primarily was in salt fish, timber, furs, flax, honey, wheat and rye, cloth and ores.[18] The furs and timber were exported from the east to the west, and clothing and later manufactured goods from England and Flanders to the eastern cities. Ore and herrings came south from Sweden.

On occasion wars were fought by the League, for example with the Danes in 1368–1370 or the Dutch in 1438–1441, over access to trade routes and markets. The League supported the Yorkists during the English War of the Roses in the fifteenth century. As time progressed cities outside of the League and merchants denied access to it in London and other cities began to envy its wealth and security. Queen Elizabeth of England expelled the League from London in 1597, for example. Earlier, free city status was curtailed or removed altogether from member cities such as Novgorod; while cities within the League began to find themselves in direct competition. New land routes opened up trade to France and inland Russia. In the sixteenth century Sweden exerted control over the Baltic, while England

16   Postan, C., *The Cambridge Economic History of Europe: Trade and Industry in the Middle Ages, Volume 2* (Cambridge: Cambridge University Press, 1987).

17   Braudel, F., *The Perspective of the World*. Vol III of Civilization and Capitalism (London: Harper & Row, 1984).

18   Girouard, M., *Cities and People* (New Haven: Yale University Press, 1985). See Chapter 1, 'The Revival of the West'.

and Denmark were locked in a trade war with the Dutch. The combined effects of these trends and events caused the League to dissipate by the late seventeenth century.

Put crudely, trade was destroyed by politics and expansionist monarchies, and the rise of the Dutch merchants. Only nine members attended the last formal meeting of the League in 1669. Nevertheless, as can still be seen in the architecture of the time, the Hanseatic League generated great wealth. The artists at the time of the League's zenith were Bosch, Durer, Grunewald, the Holbeins and later Rubens.

Trade, of course, continued but the Baltic routes were to some extent eclipsed by the opening up of sea routes to the New World and Indonesia, largely controlled by the Dutch, the Portuguese, the Spanish and the British. Amsterdam, London and Lisbon became the greatest ports, and the gravity of wealth creation itself shifted west – in the UK to Glasgow, Liverpool and Bristol and away from Leith, Newcastle and Ipswich. Memories of the Hanseatic League dimmed as Germany was in the throes of its wars of unification and France subjected most of mainland Europe.

With the fall of Communism in the east, trading opportunities that had lain dormant for 250 years began to re-connect, initially as an exercise in tourism promotion. However, the real impetus was generated from the early 1990s when a Finish company, Elcoteq, opened a plant in Estonia. Admittedly, the primary aim was to lower production costs as wages in Estonia were one-tenth of those in Finland, but Elcoteq also realised that the workforce was well-educated and that Finns and Estonians share similarities in culture and language.

The Estonian government then abolished tariffs on imports. Trade mushroomed and for the rest of the 1990s, economic growth was achieved at an annual rate of 5 per cent. The initial opening up to foreign investment continued and led to a surge in wealth creation and affluence. Estonia was now attracting more inward investment than any other European country per capita, after Hungary and the Czech Republic. However, since joining the European Union Estonia has been forced to introduced new tariffs, quotas and subsidies.[19] To bring us right up to date, Estonia has fared badly during the recession of 2008–2009, with a property market collapse, international trade that slowed, and an economy that shrank by 14 per cent in 2009. To compound things, Estonia is deciding whether or no to join the Euro, although it must be alarmed at what is happening to Greece and Ireland.

Seen in a slightly larger context, Estonia is now part of a regional industry cluster specialising in mobile communications and related technologies and services. This is led by larger firms such as Nokia and Ericsson and encompasses geographically parts of Sweden, Estonia, Finland and Denmark. The Baltic is once again a place of great trade and innovation, although these days its products are exported globally.

---

19   Norberg, J., *In Defence of Global Capitalism* (Washington, DC: Cato Institute, 2003), p. 144.

There are many lessons from all of this: the rediscovery of old trading partners; the export of investment to lower labour-cost countries bringing growth in wealth creation to all concerned; the building up of a high-tech cluster based initially on mobile communications; the use of designers and artists in fashioning products and devices, but also in providing content; the role of the arts and the good life in adding to the attractiveness of the Hansas as places to live and to invest in. One day this might all be swept away by changing economic trends and conditions of trade, but one would hope that the New Hanseatic League will be flexible and far-sighted enough not to implode as did its predecessor in the seventeenth century.

Chinese East Coast Cities: Isolation and Trade

Chinese cities such as Hong Kong, Shanghai and Shenzhen are today pre-eminent trading centres, but this was not always the case. Despite the opening up of trade routes to the West in the thirteenth century, China from the mid seventeenth century reverted for almost 400 years to its traditional Imperial rule of bureaucratic and centralised government. This totalising approach was damaged first of all by the Opium Wars of the nineteenth century, and then by totalitarian Communism for most of the second half of the twentieth century. Ironically, the long-term impact of the Opium Wars was to help these cities achieve economic growth following the re-introduction of capitalism from the 1980s.

In the late thirteenth century the Venetian merchant explorer Marco Polo travelled to Mongolian China with his father Niccolo and uncle Maffeo, arriving at the court of the great Kublai Khan in 1275. They stayed for 17 years. During this time, and in the years that followed, China opened up to trade from the West, including with Scandinavia, Greece, Hungary, Asia Minor and Arabia. This was the beginning of trade between China and other merchant cities and empires.

One interesting question is how did China come to have so many goods to export to Europe? Jacobs argues that China's cities – some 1,700 of them – had already developed as city regional economies.[20] Indeed, well before the unification of Imperial China, China had a very sophisticated culture, languages and philosophy. It had developed expertise in silk and weaving, pottery and ceramics, metallurgy, boats and chariots, bells, fishing nets, agricultural tools and much more. China also had currencies, codified laws and scientific theories. China's cities had flourished over the centuries prior to the Mongol invasion, notably during the Tang Dynasty.

An uprising led by Chu Yuan-chang overthrew the Mongols in the mid fourteenth century, establishing the Ming Dynasty in the process. The Ming Dynasty at first ushered in another great Chinese Enlightenment and maintained trade with other countries. During this time the grand canal linking Peking to the sea at Huangzhou was completed, and Peking itself was rebuilt as the nation's capital. However, later Emperors, notably Zhu Zhanji, ordered the end of overseas

---

20   Jacobs, J., *Cities and the Wealth of Nations* (New York: Random House, 1984).

trade, and returned China to the traditional ways of bureaucratic governance, headed by the Imperial Secretariat and Six Ministries for personnel, revenue, rites, war, justice and public works.[21]

The Ming Dynasty died out – the last Emperor hanged himself – to be replaced by the Manchu, a tribe from the far northeast, in 1644. The Manchu governed China in a highly centralised manner, dividing the country into 18 provinces. The Manchu were eventually overthrown and replaced by the Qing Dynasty, seen culturally as a golden age. But economic decline continued. During the Qing Dynasty a strip of coast 700 miles long and 30 miles wide was razed and the population forcibly moved inland. The penalty for trading with foreigners was death. Not surprisingly, trade with the outside world became less vigorous. China lapsed into centuries of economic stagnation.

This situation continued, more or less unchanged, for a few centuries with China lagging behind the West in technology and engineering. The Portuguese, Dutch, Spaniards and the English all attempted to occupy Far Eastern territories during the seventeenth century. Macao became a commercial base for Portugal, and both the Dutch and the Spanish established fortresses on Taiwan.

The British reappeared on the scene at the end of the eighteenth century, seeking to open up trade. The Chinese were suspicious not only of foreigners but of the very concept of trade; they viewed merchants as parasites. Foreign sea trade was limited to Canton in the south, and subject to many bureaucratic restrictions.[22] By this time tea had become the national drink of England and was exported from China in large quantities. The duties on tea came to make up a substantial proportion of government revenues.[23]

In part exchange for the tea purchased from China, the English exported opium from India to China. The Qing government were more or less happy with this situation for some 30 years before becoming alarmed at the effects of opium on its people. A crackdown on the opium trade was announced in 1838. This led directly to the Opium War of 1839–1842, gun-boat diplomacy and defeat for China, although some writers[24] argue that if not opium, hostilities would have erupted over trade of any type – the point being that the Chinese had come to resent the English presence in Canton full-stop, characterising them as 'red-haired barbarians'.

Although reforms to governance and the economy were proposed from within, the bureaucracy held sway, surviving both the bloody Taiping Rebellion of 1850–1864 and the Boxer Rebellion of 1899–1901. In the end, the Qing Dynasty was dethroned by the 1912 Kuomintang Republic. By this time, Shanghai and Hong Kong especially had become great trading ports. Shanghai was one of five ports

---

21   *The Columbian History of the World* (Poole: New Orchard Editions, 1981), Chapter 28.

22   Webb, F., *A History of Hong Kong* (London: HarperCollins, 1993).

23   Ibid.

24   Ibid.

opened up to trade in the aftermath of the Opium War, the others including Ningpo, Amoy and Canton itself.

The settlement of Hong Kong became a Crown colony of the United Kingdom in 1842 under the Treaty of Nanking. Despite its difficult topography and lack of good arable land, Hong Kong offered a good harbour. That said, it was certainly not the first choice of Captain Elliot, commander of the fleet at the time; indeed it was a port in a storm, the English having been forced out of Canton. Nevertheless, Hong Kong became an entrepôt of empire, generating tremendous wealth, one of the world's foremost banking systems and rapid urban development. Its golden age – notwithstanding the late nineteenth century when trade increased more or less exponentially – was in the 1950s, 1960s and 1970s when it became a major manufacturing centre (especially in clothing and electrical engineering). The colony benefited from low taxation and achieved official growth rates of 12 per cent per annum during the 1960s. One great boost to growth was the immigration of entrepreneurs from Shanghai and cities such as Xiamen during the early 1950s as they fled Communism. Some of these would eventually invest in Kowloon and the New Territories and then Shenzhen in China. It is fair to say that but for Hong Kong, there would have been no Shenzhen.

Shanghai, meanwhile, became not only a thriving port and city economy but also a place of vice and hedonism, and architectural innovation.[25] By the 1920s, foreign capital was flooding into Shanghai, setting up new corporations in silk manufacture, chemicals, engineering and cotton mills, redeveloping the old city with 15–20 storey tower blocks, and establishing new merchant and commercial banks. Shanghai's great wealth attracted goods and crafts from rural areas and also luxury goods from around the world. Life was good for the rich Europeans who had settled in the French Concession and the International Settlement, much less luxurious for the Chinese labouring classes, but not bad either for a new generation of Chinese entrepreneurs.[26] Organised crime, prostitution, drug taking and gambling were also rife. By the mid 1920s the city's population had swollen to over three million.

But the decline of China overall continued, especially in the aftermath of the Japanese 'Twenty-one Demands' of 1915 which granted far-reaching trade concessions; while the Republic itself began to break up into 'a kaleidoscope of satrapies'.[27] To make matters worse, the Treaty of Versailles of 1919 awarded former German rights in the Shangtung peninsula to Japan, triggering the May Fourth Movement and protests across China. There followed a power struggle between Chaing Kai-shek's nationalists and the recently formed Communist

---

25   See Montgomery, J., *The New Wealth of Cities* (Aldershot: Ashgate, 2007), pp. 201–3.

26   Dong, S., *Shanghai: The Rise and Fall of a Decadent City* (New York: HarperCollins, 2000).

27   *The Columbian History of the World* (Poole: New Orchard Editions, 1981), Chapter 89, p. 1022.

Party. The Sino-Japanese War of 1937 proved decisive and after the Second World War the Communist takeover of China was complete by 1949, Chiang retreating to Taiwan.

As in the Soviet Union, Communist rule in China proved disastrous. First there was the Korean War in the early 1950s, then the failure of successive five-year economic plans, the forced collectivisation of agriculture and the state ownership of industry. In an attempt to boost agricultural production in 1958, a 'great leap forward' was declared, but this was in effect a further collectivisation that led to starvation, economic stagnation and decline. Having ruined the economy, Mao Tse-tung set about a programme of ideological indoctrination – 'The Cultural Revolution' – during which 'educated youths' were banished to the countryside for years to re-learn revolutionary ways. China lost a generation of its brightest and best, and also became more and more isolated. According to Jung Chang and Jon Halliday, Mao was responsible for the deaths of 70 million Chinese during peacetime.[28] Happily Mao died in 1976, his grip on power already weakened.

An important turning point came with the visit of President Nixon to China in 1972 and a gradual thaw in relations between China and the West. By the end of the 1970s the communist leadership, under Deng Xiaoping, realised that collectivisation was not redistributing wealth but creating poverty. Initially modest agricultural reforms were introduced allowing peasants to sell a proportion of their produce. From 1978 to 1984 agricultural production grew at an annual rate of nearly 8 per cent, generating a food surplus for the first time in almost 50 years.

Other reforms would follow: economic free zones, foreign trade, trade was permitted in the countryside, investment in capital equipment and new businesses was allowed, and foreign investment encouraged. Incomes doubled within six years, growth of 10 per cent per annum was achieved and so too was 'the biggest and fastest poverty reduction in history'.[29] Hong Kong was retained as an entrepôt following its transfer back to China in 1997, and despite the Asian financial crisis of that year and the SARS outbreak in 2003, now has the sixth highest GDP per capita in the world. It has already recovered from the 2008–2009 recession, with growth of 7.3 per cent over the first half of 2010, with exports growing 36 per cent over the year to August 2010.

Shanghai has likewise enjoyed an economic and a development boom, after years of being deliberately held back by Mao (who resented Shanghai for its role in defeating the Communists in the late 1920s and early 1930s). Shanghai was left out of the first round of economic reforms in the 1980s, but was given the go-ahead by Deng Xiaoping in 1992. Pudong was established as an enterprise zone (in 1990). Following this, Shanghai achieved growth of 13 per cent per annum for the rest of the decade. Per capita income is the highest in China. This wealth has been built on Shanghai's role as a port and clearinghouse, linking internal cities and

---

28   Chang, Jung and Halliday, Jon, *Mao: The Unknown Story* (London: Jonathan Cape, 2005).

29   World Bank, *World Development Report 2001/2002*, p. 202.

regions to the coastal arc, and with international trade. Shanghai is now the world's second largest port. Large Western manufacturing concerns such as Volkswagen, GM, Phillips and Coca-Cola have opened manufacturing bases in Shanghai, raw materials coming from the Baoshan iron and steel works. High-tech zones have been established in Jinqiao, Zhangjiang (bio-medicine) and Caohejing. However, this astonishing growth has brought with it pollution, poor air quality and pressure on supplies of clean water. Some 20 million square metres of old buildings have been demolished to make way for skyscrapers and business parks; instead of the fine grain and human scale of the city's traditional townscape, Shanghai's planners seem fixated with large urban projects and Modernism.

The irony is that this story of opening up trade to the West and wealth creation began with the Polos in the thirteenth century but then was extinguished by the late Ming and Qing Dynasties. The Opium Wars did great damage to China as an empire and its traditional civilisation but they showed a way forward based on economic development and trade. Communism has simply held back this process by about 50 years.

Amsterdam: New Wealth and Old Masters

The question that puzzles many about the Dutch Old Masters of the seventeenth century is why such a small country should have experienced such an astonishing flowering of artistic creativity.[30] The answer, of course, was trade. Indeed, as Mark Girouard puts it, 'what impressed contemporaries about Amsterdam was that it was a city entirely dedicated to making money ... commerce was inescapable'.[31] Trade and the wealth creation it produced had lifted the city's population from about 20,000 in the mid sixteenth century to 200,000 by the end of the seventeenth century. By this time Dutch ships had become the chief carriers of goods to Europe, and most of this trade was centred on the docks, warehouses and exchanges of Amsterdam.

During the late sixteenth century, the Dutch East India Company, founded in 1609, was trading with the Far East, the Cape of Good Hope and Indonesia. Later, the West Indies Company would sail to West Africa and the Americas, creating colonies in Surinam, the Antilles and Nieuw-Amsterdam (later New York). Amsterdam as a trading port had initially been part of the Hanseatic League, which it had joined in 1369. By 1650 Amsterdam had a fleet of around 15,000 vessels, about 60 per cent of the entire European fleet, and manned by some 50,000 sailors.[32]

---

30   This material on Amsterdam was first published in my book *The New Wealth of Cities* (Aldershot: Ashgate, 2007).

31   Girouard, M., *Cities and People* (New Haven: Yale University Press, 1985), Chapter 8.

32   Jones, E., *Metropolis: The World's Great Cities* (Oxford: Oxford University Press, 1990), p. 55.

This pattern of trade created great wealth in Amsterdam, and also opportunities to manufacture using previously unavailable ingredients. For example the established wool industry developed into a thriving linen, and later silk, industry. Shipbuilding itself was a major industry, and oriental spices and crops gave rise to new forms of local consumption, in coffee, tea, spices and oils. Diamonds imported from South Africa gave rise to the gemstone industry that still exists today. In addition, new pigments were discovered by grinding various spices and exotic plants.

As wealth grew, the city attracted the finest craftsmen from all over Europe, and the wealthy merchants began to commission furniture, objects and art.[33] In comparison with other countries at the time, Holland, a Republic since 1588 when it broke away from Spanish rule, was considered a tolerant society. Although Calvinism was the official religion, Catholics were free to observe their religion (if not to hold public office). Jews were made more welcome than in other countries, and indeed many had come from Portugal, Poland and Germany. So free was Holland considered, that the French philosopher Rene Descartes moved there in 1631. A new class of wealthy bankers, manufacturers, shippers and merchants grew rapidly, and it was these people who would create the demand for a school of secular painting. This was Holland's Golden Age.[34] The arts flourished. By the mid sixteenth century, the Low Countries had more painters working in a greater variety of genres than many other countries combined.[35] Paintings would become the most common objects of art. The subject matter would range from portraits and genre scenes to landscapes and still life. Ways of seeing and ways of painting advanced, in part to keep pace with demand for new work.

The Dutch and Flemish traditions in painting had a pedigree dating back to the early fifteenth century. Indeed, at the same time as the Renaissance in Florence, the Netherlands was having a renascence all of its own. The leading artists were van Eyck and van der Weyden, both noted for highly realistic scenes and great attention to detail. They were able to do this because they had perfected a technique of mixing ground-up colours with oils to create oil paints, and because these dried more slowly than the previous, fast-drying egg-based (tempera) paints the artists were able build up layers of fine detail. Breugel would later, in the mid sixteenth century, begin to paint landscapes and country peasants as he saw them, instead of the idealised style of the Italians. This gave rise to a tradition of humane non-religious art that continued in Holland and Flanders for 400 years.[36] It was from this tradition that artists such as Rembrandt, Vermeer, Hals, Maes, Jan Steen and Cuyp would emerge.

---

33   Braudel, F., *The Perspective of the World.* Vol III of Civilization and Capitalism (London: Harper & Row, 1984).

34   Schama, S., *The Embarrassment of Riches: An Interpretation of Dutch Culture in the Golden Age* (Berkeley: University of California Press, 1987).

35   Priem, R., *Dutch Masters* (Melbourne: National Gallery of Victoria, 2005), p. xxxi.

36   Bolton, R., *A Brief History of Painting* (London: Robinson, 2004), pp. 69–94.

The majority of Dutch artists of the Golden Age did not receive regular commissions from either public bodies or private citizens. Rather, painters were organised in guilds, established to afford some measure of financial security in hard times, and also to prevent artists from other cities competing locally. The guilds had developed from the thirteenth century, and operated an extensive apprentice system that trained studio painters until they reached the level of 'master'. By and large, this meant that the artists were unable to sell their works outside of their local city, although there were exceptions in the case of Hals and Rembrandt during the peak of their fame. Artists were allowed to sell direct to individual members of the public visiting their studios, but exhibitions and auctions were organised by the guild. To get around this, many artists took to giving paintings to creditors, in exchange for settling debts with innkeepers and art dealers such as Hendrick van Uylenburgh. Some artists attempted to become dealers themselves, but most failed. So while there was indeed a great demand for art, making a living was not easy.

It was not only in the fine arts that the northern Netherlands excelled. A tradition in majolica pottery had developed with the arrival of a number of Italian potters in the early sixteenth century. This would eventually lead to the creation of a major ceramics industry, as the local potters succeeded in responding to the threat from imported Chinese porcelain. By using new techniques and improved artistry and design, the potters were able to make their majolica thinner, the new product being branded as 'Dutch Porcelain'. The centres of this new industry were Delft and Haarlem, and during the period of the civil war in China (1644–1647) delftware filled the gap in the market brought about by the collapse in porcelain trade.

City planning at the time reflected the fact that people would need to live and work in much the same space. The merchants built fine houses for themselves, set along canals and around squares, while many guildhalls, markets, exchanges and even warehouses occupied good locations. Amsterdam's urban character had not changed greatly since the fifteenth century, and the old city grew within the confines of the Singel canal, which in turn had transformed from a system of ditch fortifications to an urban waterway. But the rapid growth of the Golden Age would necessitate a city expansion. In the seventeenth century, a large area to the west of the city, now known as Jordaan and Leyden, was laid out as a residential and workers district, with small factory buildings, tanneries, mills and dye works.[37]

By the middle of the seventeenth century, the economy of the northern Netherlands was in decline, occasioned by the long slump in the European economy of that time. Competition from England and France had driven down cargo prices, and the Dutch were unable to compete with the now more innovative English shippers. The end came with the 'Year of Disasters', 1672, when the Republic waged war on France, England and the bishops of Munster and Cologne. The Golden Age was over, and with it the extraordinary creativity of the Dutch Masters.

---

37   Kostof, S., *The City Assembled* (London: Thames and Hudson, 1992), p. 92.

Tokyo: The Art of the Floating World

The Great Wave off Kanagawa by Katsushika Hokusai is one of the most recognisable works of art in human history. Part of the eighteenth- and early nineteenth-century art movement Ukiyo-e in Japan, it has influenced artists and musicians ever since and remains, of itself, surprisingly modern and contemporary. It is for me a metaphor for trade, economic development and artistic development, merged into one. In Tokyo's case it portended what was to come, for Kanagawa itself was to become the centre of Japan's electronics industry.

The history of Tokyo stretches back some 400 years. Originally named Edo, the city replaced Kyoto as Japan's capital under the Tokugawa Shogunate in 1603. Edo grew into a large city with a population of over a million by the mid eighteenth century, although the Emperor resided in Kyoto. The Edo Period lasted for nearly 260 years until the Meiji Restoration in 1868, when the Tokugawa Shogunate ended and Imperial rule was restored. The Emperor moved to Edo, which was renamed Tokyo in 1868.[38]

Edo's early growth and prosperity was based on the internal trade between towns, castle towns and market towns, and a system of roads that connected them. Trade was in artisan goods, cloth, crops and livestock. But this came to an abrupt end with the unification of Japan in 1603 under the Shogunate, a rigid system of governance based on military strength and a fixed hierarchy. The merchant class were unable to travel as before as contact with the outside world was strictly forbidden. Japan began a long period of isolation that would slowly come to an end following the US expedition under Matthew Perry that opened Japan up to trade with the modern world. Economic development during the Tokugawa period was characterised by increased domestic shipping of commodities, an expansion of domestic commerce, a diffusion of trade and craft industries, rising agricultural production and the spread of rural handicrafts. Edo became an important centre for food production and urban consumer goods: tea, tobacco, wax, indigo, salt, knives, swords, pottery, lacquer ware, silk, cotton, soy sauce, sake, paper, stone cutting, medicines and herbs. By the mid eighteenth century, Edo had a population of more than one million.

Tradition has it that the merchants of Edo turned to kabuki theatre, sumo, the beauty of nature and brothels to fill their time.[39] According to Buddhist tradition these 'lower form' of pleasures are known as 'the floating world'. Ukiyo-e art represents and records this period of Japanese society, and especially urban life and the 'pleasure quarters' of Yoshiwara and New Yoshiwara in Edo. Prints of famous actors, courtesans and explicit sexual activity were very popular. Ukiyo-e was a popular cultural form of its day, but now is considered high art. The art form was affordable because prints could be produced easily from the blocks,

---

38   Kanagawa Prefectural Government, *The History of Kanagawa* (Yokohama, 1985).

39   Benson, Marcus, 'The Sensual World of Ukiyo-e Art', *The Australian Financial Review*, 9–11 May 2008, p. L18.

and gained in popularity with then invention of nishiki-e technique by Hishikawa Moronubo, allowing for the production of full colour prints. Moronubo was the first recognised master of the Edo period.

The two great masters were Hokusai and Hiroshige, both of whom produced landscapes as well as urban scenes. Hiroshige was born in Edo in 1797, and is best-known for several series of works depicting the Japanese landscape – notably *100 Views of Famous Place in and Around Edo*. Hokusai[40] produced *36 Views of Mount Fuji* and this includes *The Great Wave off Kanagawa*. *The Great Wave* is a seascape with Mount Fuji in the background. The wave itself is depicted as a claw, about to engulf some fishermen. Hokusai studied Dutch techniques of printmaking, more precisely etching.

Ukiyo-e itself began to adapt as modern influences came to Japan, but it was eventually replaced by photography in the early twentieth century. By the end of the Second World War, Ukiyo-e was in decline,[41] but has mustered a comeback since the 1990s. Less well known perhaps is that Ukiyo-e had a great impact on Impressionism and post-Impressionism in Europe. Monet, for example, lined the walls of Giverny with woodblock prints, while Van Gogh copied and reinterpreted some of Hiroshige's works, notably the *Sudden Shower over the Ohashi Bridge*. It is arguable that the simple lines and structure of Ukiyo-e also helped shape Modernism, certainly early Cubism.[42] Edgar Degas was more drawn to the metropolitan Ukiyo-e, the images of geishas especially. This influence was known for a time as *Japonisme* or *Japonaiserie*. Beyond art, Ukiyo-e influenced the architecture of Frank Lloyd Wright who became an avid collector and dealer. It is said that *The Great Wave* inspired Debussy's great orchestrated *Images*, particularly *La Mer* (1905). It is also true to some extent that Japan's current expertise in cartoons, comic books and graphic arts is born of the Ukiyo-e tradition and methods. The cartoons industry was also important in the development of video and computer games and software.

The Edo period thus developed a network of burgeoning urban centres, a relatively well-educated elite, strong government, productive agriculture and a national infrastructure of roads. Although trade was restricted to domestic centres, enough prosperity was created to generate a wealthy merchant class and a banking system. The emergence of Ukiyo-e as a quintessentially distinct art form was due to demand from these merchants and bankers.

Barely 50 years after the restoration of the Meiji Emperor and the opening up of trade with the West, Tokyo had become a centre of a railway network, and had acquired a modern port, factories and department stores.[43] Later it would become

40   Lane, Richard, *Hokusai: Life and Work* (New York: E. P. Dutton, 1989).

41   Ishiguro, Kazuo, *An Artist of the Floating World* (London: Faber & Faber, 1986).

42   Lambourne, Lionel, *Japonisme: Cultural Crossings Between Japan and the West* (London: Phaidon Press, 2005).

43   Girouard, M., *Cities and People* (New Haven: Yale University Press, 1985), p. 333.

one of the world's great centres of electronics and the computer industry,[44] riding the wave of the post-war boom and the emergence of new technologies. But this happened in Tokyo rather than, say, Kyoto, for the simple reason that Edo had already developed wealth-creating expertise and traditions.

Lisbon: Rebuilding and Economic Recovery

On 1 November 1755, All Saints Day, one of the most devastating earthquakes in modern history struck Lisbon. Scientific measurement of earthquake magnitudes did not yet exist but its magnitude was most likely between 8.5 and 9.0 on the modern Richter scale.[45] At that time Lisbon was a city of some 300,000 souls, grown wealthy from trade with Brazil, especially in silver and spices.[46]

The earthquake began several hours after dawn. For about 10 minutes during midmorning, the earth shook, rolled and collapsed. The quake itself levelled numerous major buildings in the port area, and the royal palace was destroyed; 85 per cent of Lisbon's buildings were destroyed, including famous palaces and libraries. Because of the holy day, churches were filled with morning worshippers, who were crushed under the weight of collapsing walls and roofs.

Frequent aftershocks caused further damage. Fires sprang up, and a wind from the northeast helped to blow the various blazes together into a general conflagration. The fires destroyed the rich contents of churches and palaces, consuming paintings, manuscripts, books and tapestries.[47]

The epicentre was located many miles out to sea. The collapse of the seabed triggered a vast tsunami that hurtled towards southern Portugal and Spain and across Gibraltar into Morocco. In a final assault, the tsunami struck, a sequence of tidal waves, some towering over 20 feet.[48] Within a few morning hours, quake, fire and flood had destroyed one of the major ports and great cities of Europe.

The death toll was estimated as being as high as 100,000. Fear, hunger, looting and disease followed. Thousands fled the city, blocking roads and passages. Food could not enter the city, and countless of the injured were left to fend for themselves. The core of the city was left virtually uninhabitable. No exact tally of the total losses was ever made, but it was estimated that approximately 10% of Portugal's wealth was consumed by the devastation.

---

44 Hall, P., *Cities in Civilisation* (London: Weidenfeld and Nicolson, 1998), Chapter 15.

45 Brooks, Charles B., *Disaster at Lisbon: The Great Earthquake of 1755* (Long Beach, CA: Shangton Longley Press, 1994).

46 Girouard, M., *Cities and People* (New Haven: Yale University Press, 1985), p. 144.

47 Kendrick, T. D., *The Lisbon Earthquake* (London: Methuen, 1956).

48 Chester, D. K., 'The 1755 Lisbon Earthquake', *Progress in Physical Geography*, 25(3), 2001, 363–383.

Rebuilding Lisbon became the responsibility of Sebastião José de Carvalho e Melo, the principal minister of King Joseph I and the future Marquês de Pombal.[49] Pombal gave first priority to stopping the spread of disease: 'Bury the dead and feed the living'. Bodies not burned in fires were collected on boats and sunk in the Tagus River. The army was drafted in to put out fires, clear streets and passages of rubble, and to set up field tents and food kitchens. Anyone caught looting was summarily executed. Prices for food and building materials were fixed to prevent profiteering.

Pombal began to prepare for the reconstruction of the city within a matter of weeks following the earthquake. Having rejected the option of building a new city on another site, Pombal then set about planning the city's reconstruction, paying particular attention to improving its layout.[50] Lisbon's old, twisting, narrow streets were replaced, especially in the flat central part of the city – the Baixa – with wide, straight streets that crossed at right angles in a grid pattern. A series of spacious plazas was also created. Pombal's 'clean slate' option produced six detailed plans designed largely by military engineers. Pombal's goal was to create a city that reflected the new values of the Enlightenment. The city was to reflect a society in which the citizen, the merchant and the bureaucrat took precedence over the crown, Church and nobility. The reconstruction overall was financed by gold from Brazil, trade with other European countries and a 4 per cent tax on manufacturing.

Pombal insisted that all structures must be built to officially approved standards. Construction was undertaken by a group of skilled military engineers, headed by the veteran officer Manuel de Maia, who organised the planning and rebuilding. Buildings were prefabricated, and the sizes of doors, windows and walls were standardised. To protect against future earthquakes, building frames were made of wood that could sway under pressure without breaking. The Pombaline Baixa is thus one of the first examples of earthquake resistant construction. Architectural models were tested by having troops march around them to simulate an earthquake. Notable features of Pombaline structures include the 'Pombaline cage', a symmetrical wood-lattice framework aimed at distributing earthquake force, and inter-terrace walls that are built higher than roof timbers to reduce fire contagion. The style of these new structures, a kind of simplified or plain Baroque, came to be known as *Pombaline*. The Lisbon earthquake changed urban planning and architecture.

Because of this response to the earthquake, Lisbon came to be among the best-planned and best-constructed cities in eighteenth-century Europe. It pre-dated Edinburgh's New Town by over 20 years. The modernised port imported a high volume of manufactured goods, most of them from Great Britain, which had

---

49   Maxwell, Kenneth, *Pombal: Paradox of the Enlightenment* (Cambridge: Cambridge University Press, 1995).

50   Ockman, Joan, *Out of Ground Zero: Case Studies in Urban Reinvention* (New York: Prestel, 2002), Chapter 1.

already begun to industrialise. Much of the wealth that Portugal received in the form of Brazilian gold thus helped to capitalise the earliest stages of the Industrial Revolution.

There were also philosophical reverberations, not only in Portugal but all around Europe. The earthquake struck during the early years of the Enlightenment or *Age of Reason*. Thinkers of the Enlightenment argued that the Lisbon earthquake needed to be studied not as a supernatural event but as a natural one. Voltaire famously wrote a long poem immediately after the earthquake before going on to write *Candide*. Immanuel Kant wrote a series of three essays on the causes of earthquakes. Pombal himself commissioned a major survey of the earthquake, its causes and effects, and this is acknowledged as the beginning of the science of seismology. Rousseau, in a letter to Voltaire, claimed that the high death toll was due to too many people living within the close quarters of the city, arguing that country life is preferable to urban living.

Pombal – his title was only granted in 1770 – remains a great hero in Portugal, yet his contribution to city planning is often overlooked or under-rated. To be sure, his approach is an *example extraordinaire* of top-down planning where little deviation from his plans was countenanced. He explicitly rejected past values (religious orthodoxy) and urban forms in order that the city should reflect the most modern thought possible. Lisbon was largely redesigned by an autocratic leader and his handpicked military engineers. The result was not only effective but beautiful. An enforced adoption of Enlightenment principles to city governance and urban planning produced the most modern and architecturally advanced capital in the world.

Just as important, Portugal's economy was able to recover from utter devastation – in much the same way as West German cities after 1945 – but without aid from the United States. Portugal recaptured her trade with colonies in South America, the East Indies and South China.

Vienna: End of an Empire

The reason once-important trading cities lose their prowess lies in a loss of dynamism, creativity and entrepreneurship. Put crudely, they cease to trade as potently as they once had. This can be seen in the case of the Japanese Shogunate, the cities of Imperial China and cities that were once part of the Hanseatic League. In some cases, this comes about from changes in the pattern of trade, loss of markets, changes in demand, the opening up of new trade routes and so on. Another reason – hinted at in the case of Edo and Imperial China but not often referred to directly – is where a city effectively turns its back on trade, preferring to see itself as a seat of Imperial power. Vienna is a case in point.

On the eve of the outbreak of the First World War, Austria-Hungary remained one of the most powerful empires of its or any other day. In Vienna, it had a capital of great sophistication and cultural innovation, and this was a city in which new ideas of psychoanalysis would take hold. By 1919 Austria's power had all but disappeared and the once great centre that was Vienna was simply one of many small European capitals. What went wrong?

Robert Musil's masterpiece[51] describes the long, slow decline of Vienna as seen through the eyes of Ulrich, a rich ex-soldier, seducer and scientist, 'a man without qualities'. The book is set in the Vienna of 1913 where attention is focused on the 70th anniversary of the accession of Emperor Franz Joseph, seemingly oblivious of the gathering storm that became the First World War, and the death of the Austro-Hungarian Empire. Vienna was too busy waltzing to realise that this was the last waltz.

> Time was on the move ... But nobody knew where time was headed. And it was not always clear what was up or down, what was going backward or forward. "No matter what you do" the man without qualities thought with a shrug, "... it doesn't make the slightest difference".[52]

The final chapter of *The Man Without Qualities* is entitled 'A Great Event is in the Making, But No One Has Noticed'. The characters are too busy conducting their affairs to take the looming war seriously. We could be harsh, and conclude that a combination of easy living and romantic ennui had removed enthusiasm and spirit from the ruling classes, themselves increasingly vain and narcissistic. But surely there is more?

Over the next five years, Austro-Hungary would lose its empire, but even worse was to follow. In 1938 Austria was 'annexed' to Hitler's Germany and ceased to exist as a state. Most of Vienna's Jewish population was driven away or exterminated. One such was the classical scholar and early psychoanalyst David Oppenheim, a friend both of Freud and Alfred Adler who famously fell out with each other during meetings of Freud's Wednesday Group. Oppenheim and his wife Amalie were 'resettled' to a gehtto in Czechoslovakia, where David would die from illness and malnutrition in 1943. His children survived and one of his daughters made it to Australia. She was the mother of author and philosopher Peter Singer.[53] Singer tells of the early twentieth century – the time of the man without qualities – as a period of intellectual debate amongst a Jewish populous that was notably secular. 'The gang', as Freud referred to his Vienna Psychoanalytic Society, were mostly Jewish and liberal and bourgeois. Freud confessed privately that he found little inspiration in his colleagues, or from Viennese café society.

Vienna was the seat of the Hapsburgs from 1278 when Rudolf I took control over the Austrian lands after his victory over Ottokar II of Bohemia. Despite several wars and invasion, including by the Ottomans in 1589 and 1683 and Napolean in

---

51   Musil, R., *The Man Without Qualities* (London: Picador, 1997).

52   Ibid., p. 7.

53   Singer, P., *Pushing Time Away: My Grandfather and the Tragedy of Jewish Vienna* (Sydney: HarperCollins, 2003).

1805 and 1809, Vienna remained the centre of the Austro-Hungary Empire until 1918. As a royal court city, Vienna attracted artists and musicians from all over Europe, particularly in the eighteenth and early nineteenth centuries. The city's population expanded most rapidly during the second half of the nineteenth century, and there were 2,031,000 inhabitants by 1910.

Vienna experienced a renewed surge in artistic creativity at the end of the nineteenth century. A new group of young painters, musicians and poets emerged, *Jung Wien*, named after *Die Jung* political movement of the 1870s. The writers included Arthus Schnitzler, who influenced Freud, Karl Kraus, Hugo von Hofmannsthal and Robert Musil. They had in common a rejection of bourgeois moralism and favoured 'sociological truth and psychological – especially sexual – openness'. They shared a certain disdain for what they considered the superficial narcissism and trivial nature of Viennese society:[54] such things as cultivation, civilised pleasures, good company, manners and public social life. Vienna, in their eyes, was too comfortable, too bourgeois and somehow decaying.

Of course, the Great War was a hammer blow for the Austro-Hungarian Empire. On 12 November 1918, the Republic of *Deutsch-Österreich*, or German-Austria, was proclaimed. But, worse, like Germany and other parts of Europe, Austria became a fertile breeding ground for social reform and accompanying ideological movements – Progressivism, Socialism, Communism, National Socialism, all of which were intent on tearing down the old bourgeois societies in order to promote the 'greater good'. Instead, they plunged Europe into darkness. Robert Musil may have been right to criticise and parody Viennese society of 1913, but the truth is that the everyday trivia of coffee, cakes, salons and affairs is greatly to be preferred over reforming zealotry.

There are two possible morals to this tale. One is that Viennese society was indeed decaying, rotten at the core, collapsing in on its own self-centredness, as argued by the *Jung Wien*. Certainly, the Viennese seem not to have noticed that the world was changing all too rapidly, and that for all their cultural sophistication, they somehow lacked essential qualities or principles. The other is that, by challenging traditional values and morality, *Jung Wien* actively contributed to a moral and cultural decline similar, say, to the 1960s in Britain. The old ways of doing things, the wisdom and proprieties built up over many generations, were rudely swept aside. That *Jung Wien* was a period of great artistic creativity is not any doubt, but it was followed by and perhaps helped cause a collapse of Viennese society.

And so a city that was once the seat of a sprawling empire of 50 million people is now the small capital of a nation of less than eight million. Vienna has admittedly maintained a façade worthy of its former glory, particularly the architectural masterpieces of the historic inner city core. And, of course, it still has the coffee houses. Music is also an important part of Vienna's culture: Mozart, Beethoven and Schubert and the waltz. Indeed, it is this cultural history that underpins the city's

---

54   Hall, P., *Cities in Civilization* (London: Weidenfeld and Nicolson, 1998), Chapter 5, 'The City as Pleasure Principle'.

important tourism sector. Each year the city records some 3.3 million arrivals, generating an annual turnover of around EUR 2.5 billion. That is equivalent to about 5 per cent of Vienna's total GDP. The state-owned theatres alone employ several thousand people. Some 75 per cent of workers employed in Vienna work in the service sector, including banking, insurance and business tourism. The main manufacturing sectors are metal production and processing, food processing and printing, mostly for local and domestic consumption.

Unlike other great capital cities such as London or Paris or Copenhagen, Vienna was never a commercial or trading city, or a site for manufacturing. The goods that serviced the Empire were produced in other cities and regions, notably in Bohemia with its expertise in cloth production, and later its coalfields and steel-works. Because of this, Vienna has never really had a dynamic economy; it is not a self-generating city economy. Although it had at least two great artistic golden ages and periods of Baroque and classical city building, it is perhaps not so very different from Canberra or Washington DC as a city of government more so than commerce.

Commentary

The examples in this chapter were intended to demonstrate the dynamic processes by which cities grow, trade, prosper, adopt new technologies, find new industries to excel in and specialise. The examples all tell a similar story of growth and, in some cases, re-invention and new growth. A similar trajectory has been followed by scores of cities across the Western world and within market economies wherever they are found. Some places do better than others, and the telling difference seems to be the willingness to adapt, to remain an open system, trade and make necessary political decisions in a timely manner. In a way, the striking thing is the similarity between cities where successful adaptation has occurred. A few examples illustrate what happens when city economies do not innovate and diversify, and fail to develop patterns of local consumption, notably the Imperial Chinese cities, Edo under the Shogunate and Vienna.

Very often, almost always, the very same cities that experience waves of great prosperity also are the places in which major artistic breakthroughs occur. For the past 1,000 years or so, certain cities have come to be associated with great periods of wealth creation, innovation and technology, and also artistic breakthroughs. The inhabitants of these cities – the city fathers, the merchant class and, later, the growing middle class – developed an aesthetic sensibility, which led them to seek art because it was beautiful and satisfying for its own sake as well as for any benefit it might bring oneself or others, such as having a portrait painted by a Dutch Master. This underscores the importance of the sense of taste in the development of art forms and movements.

In this way, commerce and economic progress are artistically and ethically beneficent. Wealth creation, knowledge, and our humanity, are linked. This is most observable during a golden age. But without preceding and at times contemporaneous waves of wealth creation, great movements in the arts would not have occurred. The great creative milieux of Western civilisation and capitalism – Venice, Florence, Edinburgh, London, Amsterdam, Paris and Lisbon – all of these great cities had a period of great wealth creation and intellectual development, a golden age. They became wealthy and cultured at much the same time. They applied knowledge to the economic, philosophical, scientific and cultural questions of the day. They prospered as a result, as long as they didn't forget the importance of new work and endeavour, and trade.

Chapter 6
Growth and Decline:
Part II – Industrial Capitalism
and the New Economy

I will (tell) the story as I go of small cities no less than great. Most of those which were great once are small today; and those which in my own lifetime have grown to greatness, were small enough in the old days.

Herodotus, *The Histories*

Herodotus was writing of the great cities of Egypt and Mesopotamia he visited in the fifth century BC, for example the walled city of Uruk, Babylon and Nippur. Almost all have since declined, in most cases thousands of years ago. Some scholars[1] argue that the growth of Hellenic culture and city building, and thus also Ancient Rome, can be traced to the development of the very cities Herodotus writes of. In turn, the Greek city states and Rome itself would stagnate and decline. It seems that, over the course of time, the influence and dominance of particular cities waxes and wanes. In the ancient world this was often to do with Imperial wars of conquest, but also because of shifts in trade and commerce. In our more recent history, cities have continued to prosper and at times decline.

The great period of city growth was during the nineteenth century. This was caused by rapid economic growth and two surges in wealth creation, in the early part of the century and again from about 1845 until the 1890s. People flocked from the countryside to the cities, a great number of which experienced phenomenal population growth. There was another great period of city expansion in the early part of the twentieth century until the Second World War, and yet another in the post-war period. These episodes of city growth coincide with the four Kondratieff waves, as already discussed. This is no surprise, as the great waves of growth are caused by the development of new products and services – mostly in cities – and by trade between city regions.

Growth, then, to repeat, depends on trade between city regions, that is to say clusters and networks of economic activity that exist in real places. This growth is driven or led by new industries that are the product of technological advances and innovation. This innovation is a creative process that takes hold only in certain places that encourage the commercialization of new products and processes, and artistic and scientific experimentation and adaptation. To square the argument, those cities that are flexible, economically diverse, adaptable to changing

---

1   Mumford, L., *The City in History* (New York: Harvest, 1961), p. 137.

circumstances, innovative and creative are the cities that achieve long episodes of prosperity. Those that lose these special characteristics – that depend on one dying traditional industry – will themselves stagnate and even die. Only a few cities seem able to reinvent themselves with relative ease – London, New York, Milan, Tokyo – moving from one industrial age to another. These cities manage this because they self-generate economic activity and are less dependent on a few staple export industries.

Other cities very often have to endure a painful period of adjustment and restructuring of their economies as old industries die but the economy is insufficiently diverse to prevent rising unemployment. This fate befell many cities in the 1970s and 1980s. Examples include the potteries of Staffordshire,[2] rail and heavy engineering of Derby and Swindon, shipbuilding in Newcastle, Sunderland and Belfast, steel in Sheffield, even the cotton industry in Manchester. Sadly, this fate befell Glasgow in the second half of the twentieth century as traditional heavy industries such as shipbuilding and heavy engineering declined.

It is important to understand that production chain linkages occur within and between places – cities, clusters and regions – based on networks and patterns of trade and local consumption. In this way, cities become self-generating economic dynamos. Successful city economies diversify into all manner of goods and services, some for export, others for local consumption. They also replace some imports with goods and services supplied locally. The more diverse the city's economy, the greater prosperity will be. Yet it is clearly the case that if demand for a city's main exports collapses, economic hardship follows. Some examples will demonstrate the fact that economic growth is driven by cities along the long waves of wealth creation.

Chicago: Depot City

With over 2.8 million residents, Chicago is the largest city in the Midwestern United States and the third most populous city in the United States. The city is located in northeastern Illinois at the southwestern tip of Lake Michigan. The name 'Chicago' is from the French corruption of the Miami-Illinois word *shikaakwa*, meaning 'wild onion' or 'wild garlic'.

Chicago's history and economy are closely tied to its proximity to Lake Michigan; indeed it sits on the site of the Chicago Portage connecting the Mississippi River (and thus the Gulf of Mexico) to the Great Lakes, the St Lawrence and from there onto the Atlantic Ocean.[3] The portage was discovered in 1673 by French Canadian explorers. Prior to this the area was inhabited by a native American tribe – the Potawatomis. The first known non-indigenous permanent settler in Chicago, Jean

---

2   Rice, M., *The Lost City of Stoke-on-Trent* (London: Frances Lincoln Publishers, 2010).

3   Pacyga, Dominic A., *Chicago: A Biography* (Chicago: University of Chicago Press, 2009).

Baptiste Point du Sable, arrived in the 1780s.[4] In 1795, following the Northwest Indian War, an area that would become part of Chicago was signed over to the United States for a military post.

The city itself was founded in 1833 near the portage. Most of the early building began around the mouth of the Chicago River, laid out as 58 city blocks. To begin with, Chicago had a population of 200 people, but this would grow to 4,000 within seven years. Because of its strategic position linking the Great Lakes to the Mississippi, the city developed rapidly as an important transportation hub between the eastern and western United States, the north and the south, trans-shipping grain. The opening of the Illinois and Michigan Canal in 1848 allowed larger vessels to connect between the two waterways, sealing Chicago's role as a entrepôt. The commercial heart of the town developed along the Chicago River. Wholesale and shipping businesses occupied South Water Street, financial services located on Lake, Dearborn and Randolph streets, and lumber dealers lined the North and South Branches of the river.

This role was given a further boost when Chicago's first railway, the Galena and Chicago Union Railroad opened, also in 1848. This was the time of the long boom or upwave of the mid nineteenth century, and Chicago was by this time importing livestock from the Midwest and processing it. The great Union Stock Yards were built on 320 acres of swampland south of the city by a consortium of nine railroad in 1864, opening a year later.[5] The stockyards experienced tremendous growth, processing two million animals annually by 1870, and nine million by 1890. By the turn of the century the stockyards employed 25,000 people and produced 82 per cent of US domestic meat consumption. The invention of the refrigerated railcar allowed for transportation of meat products from Chicago to markets across the United States. The stockyards would at their peak accommodate 2,300 separate livestock pens in addition to hotels, saloons, restaurants, and offices for merchants and brokers.[6] In this way, during the 1840s, Chicago became a major grain port, and in the 1850s and 1860s Chicago's pork and beef industry expanded.

Chicago's booming economy brought migrants from rural communities and overseas immigrants. Manufacturing and retail sectors also grew rapidly to become dominant among Midwestern cities.[7] Chicago experienced some of the fastest population growth in the world. From 4,470 in 1840, the population surged to 503,000 in 1880, doubling to 1,100,000 in 1890 and again to over two million

---

4   Swenson, John W., *Jean Baptiste Point du Sable – The Founder of Modern Chicago* (Chicago: Early Chicago Inc, 1999).

5   *The Birth of the Chicago Union Stock Yards* (Chicago: Chicago Historical Society, 2001).

6   Wilson, Mark R., 'Union Stock Yard and Transit Co.', in Grossman, James R., Durkin Keating, Ann and Ruff, Janice L. (eds), *The Encyclopedia of Chicago* (Chicago: University of Chicago Press, 2004).

7   Cronon, William, *Nature's Metropolis: Chicago and the Great West* (New York: W. W. Norton, 1992 [1991]).

by 1910. (Chicago's population peaked at 3.6 million in 1950, and today is just under 2.9 million.) A great city was built in a few decades out of almost nothing. This rapid population growth was accommodated, in part, by building the world's first skyscrapers and tall buildings more generally. The Great Chicago Fire of 1871 destroyed a third of the city, allowing for rapid rebuilding, including not only tall buildings but also parks and civic amenities.[8] In 1893, Chicago hosted the World Columbian Exposition, drawing 27.5 million visitors, and is considered the most influential world's fair in history, sealing Chicago's reputation as the leading city for architecture and urban planning, including Daniel Burnham's visionary City Beautiful Chicago Plan.[9]

The 1920s saw another major expansion in industry, and the availability of jobs attracted blacks from the South. Between 1910 and 1930, the black population of Chicago increased from 44,103 to 233,903. This migration had an immense cultural impact, and it was during this time that Chicago became a centre for jazz. By this time, Chicago had a large and diverse manufacturing economy, including such products as bicycles and automobiles and electrical engineering, as well as printing and publishing. This industrial economy peaked in the mid 1970s. In the last half of the twentieth century, Chicago, like other industrial cities around the world, experienced significant amounts of industrial decentralisation and closure, as the long post-war boom ebbed. The city at one point was known as 'the capital of the rustbelt'. Chicago's metropolitan economy turned to service provision and, more recently, restructuring for the 'knowledge economy'. But, just as important, it has also diversified its manufacturing economy. Today the city's economy is dominated by a concentration of commercial offices in the Loop business district, and a widespread scatter of office parks and commercial space in the suburbs, tied closely to the expressway network.[10]

Chicago has, in this way, experienced three phases of economic development, reflecting the upwaves of the early nineteenth century, the mid to late nineteenth century and the post-war boom. Chicago grew initially as a successful merchants' town at the base of Lake Michigan, its future almost guaranteed by the opening of the Illinois & Michigan Canal and the first railroad tracks to the west. Between the Civil War and the Second World War Chicago developed into a manufacturing city of previously unknown proportions, and industry of all types spread across the urban area. Most plants located close to the waterways and railroads that crisscrossed the city. By the turn of the twentieth century – that is the third great upwave – the cheap, marshy and lakeshore lands of the South Side attracted more heavy industry.

---

8   Miller, Donald L., *City of the Century: The Epic of Chicago and the Making of America* (New York: Simon and Schuster, 1996).

9   Smith, Carl S., *The Plan of Chicago: Daniel Burnham and the Remaking of the American City* (Chicago: University of Chicago Press, 2006).

10   Brugman, J., *Welcome to the Urban Revolution: How Cities Are Changing the World* (New York: Bloomsbury Press, 2009).

Jane Jacobs argues that Chicago's growth was fuelled initially by an episode of import-replacing between 1840 and 1855. Although Chicago was a depot that handled and trans-shipped goods – mainly flour and timber shipped to European markets via the Great Lakes and on the new railroads – it also acted as a distribution point for goods coming from the east to the Midwest. Chicago was also generating its own exports, primarily machinery, shipbuilding and regional banking. But by the mid 1850s, the city was producing a large range of goods it had previously imported – clocks, medicines, furniture, stoves, kitchen utensils, tools and building components.[11] Most of this was for local regional consumption. By the late nineteenth century, Chicago was a major exporter of manufactured goods, becoming in the process a self-generating city regional economy. Because its economy was so dynamic and diverse it would later avoid the fate of single-industry cities such as Pittsburgh and Detroit where the decline of older industries led to economic stagnation.

Copenhagen: Wealth, Design, Wealth

In her book *The Economy of Cities*,[12] Jane Jacobs argues that despite periodic episodes of growth, based on sea-trade, Copenhagen was a poor and stagnant city in the eighteenth century. The city's golden age would come later, in the mid to late nineteenth century when trade with London flourished. Copenhagen had grown fitfully over a period of some 500 years, initially as a fishing village and then a seaport, owing to its position on the sound. From 1500 to the mid eighteenth century growth was modest, with long periods of stagnation. During this time, around 80 per cent of Denmark's population lived from subsistence agriculture. Between 1550 and 1650, exports made up only 5 per cent of the country's GDP, comprised mainly of oxen and grains. The period after 1650 was characterised by a prolonged slump as exports to neighbouring countries, and especially Holland, declined.

In the eighteenth century Copenhagen's economy benefited largely due to the intense traffic through the sound (and revenues and taxes). Enough wealth was created to rebuild the old city following several destructive fires in 1728 that left the city almost totally damaged and ruined. Rebuilding and reconstruction work began and was completed by 1737. This was during the reign of King Frederik V, acknowledged today as the planner and builder of Frederiksstaden, the centerpiece of which is the Amalienborg Palace. So, in architecture at least Copenhagen enjoyed a period of heightened creativity. Royal Copenhagen (Den kongelige Porcelænsfabrik) was also founded around this time, in 1775 by the chemist Frantz Heinrich Müller.

---

11   Jacobs, J., *The Economy of Cities* (New York: Vintage, 1969), p. 156.
12   Ibid.

However, the city did not experience rapid population growth at this time, and demand for Danish exports (mainly grain and livestock) declined as competition from England and Holland developed. Economic growth faltered in the late eighteenth century, so that by 1813 Denmark was bankrupt and had to cede territories to Norway and Sweden. During the eighteenth and early nineteenth centuries, a series of ill-judged military campaigns, including the Thirty Years War with Sweden, undermined the economy. In 1864, Denmark was forced to cede the Schleswig and Holstein regions to Germany. By this time, Denmark had lost most of the trade in agricultural produce to England and Holland, and there were no new streams of exports to compensate.

The change in Copenhagen's fortunes came with increased trade with London, notably exports of agricultural produce. Simply put, during the second quarter of the nineteenth century the rapid growth of London led to greater demand for food and Danish produce was in demand once more. At this time, as well as grain, Denmark was exporting animal products, mainly butter and bacon. Jacobs argues that Copenhagen was able to develop more export businesses and also to diversify its own economy through increased imports and import substitution. The city's trade, wealth and population expanded rapidly and, in the late nineteenth century, the old ramparts of the city were breached to allow the development of new residential boroughs at Vesterbro, Nørrebro and Østerbro.

However, during the post-war boom years of the 1950s Denmark's rate of GDP growth was markedly lower than the Western European average. The reason was that Denmark was still exporting predominantly agricultural products as opposed to manufactured goods. To use Sir Peter Hall's phrase, Copenhagen had to find another way to make its living. Copenhagen would grow and diversify its economy based on excellence in electronics (radio, television) that developed during the 1920s, pottery and crystal, jewellery, furniture and the design industries generally. During this time, brands such as Bang & Olufsen, Bodum and Lego were created.

From the late-nineteenth century, all manner of crafts and trades flourished, including silversmithing, jewellery and pottery, adding to an earlier specialism in cabinet-making that dated from the 1770s.[13] One of the pioneers of Danish craft and design was the silversmith Georg Jensen. Jensen was the son of a knife grinder and began his training as a goldsmith, aged 14, in 1880. He then attended the Royal Academy of Fine Arts, graduating as a sculptor in 1892. He set up a small pottery workshop in 1898 but struggled to earn a living. He turned to jewellery in 1901, opening his own silversmithy in Copenhagen in 1904. He was able to combine his knowledge of metalsmithing with his fine art training and began to design in the Art Noveau style. His works combined elegance, understatement, fine quality and beauty. Although Jensen died in 1935, his company continues to strive for artistry in design and excellence in craftsmanship. By the time of his death, Copenhagen had a reputation for good design.

---

13   Hollingsworth, A., *Modern Design* (Gibbs Smith, 2008).

The modern Danish school of design is usually dated from 1924 when the Department of Furniture was established at the Royal Danish Academy of Fine Arts by Kaare Klimt. Unlike its German counterpart, the Bauhaus, Danish design was never overtly political or socialistic but it came to be associated – at least for some – with 'social ideals ... and ... a moral and humanistic ethos'.[14] This is sometimes referred to as 'the Democratic Approach'. From the beginning the School was a Modernist project in its opposition to stylised decoration, but it was essentially a pragmatic place of work as opposed to a bed of radicalism. Its concerns were with home, family and everyday life.

The designers, of course, became educators, so that two or perhaps three generations of Danish designers studied there. The design ethos overall was one of good taste, modesty and Lutheran simplicity. The methodology was based on 'anthropometrics', empirical trial and error and human proportion and the use of traditional materials. Interesting connections began to be made between traditional handcrafting and industrial techniques. But the main emphasis was on 'craftsmanship' – pride, attention to detail and perfect execution. The 1950s and 1960s – the period of the post-war upwave – were a time of great prominence for Scandinavian design, at which point objects originally designed during the 1930s were produced in larger batches and sold worldwide. Furniture was made using new techniques of layering – for example Arne Jacobsen's *Ameise* chair designed in 1952; while Verner Panton began to design furniture composed of plastics and steel wire.

Modern architecture in Denmark is likewise cool and considered, tasteful and elegant. Arne Jacobsen is arguably the greatest exponent of Danish Modern style, both in architecture and furniture. His work includes St Catherine's College, Oxford, the Radisson SAS Royal Hotel in Copenhagen, the Royal Danish Embassy in Knightsbridge, and a number of town halls – notably the Aarhus town hall – and other buildings across Denmark. Many of his designs have become classics, notably the *Ant* chair from 1952, the *Swan* and the *Egg* and the *Number 7 Chair*, famously used in a photograph of Christine Keeler. Jacobsen also designed cutlery, dining room furniture and fittings such as door handles. He died in 1971.

Henning Larsen is another pre-eminent Danish architect. As well as office buildings and apartment blocks in Copenhagen, his work includes the University of Trondheim in Norway, university buildings in Berlin, the Danish Embassy in Riyadh, a number of houses in Milton Keynes and an extension to the famed Louisiana Art Museum north of Copenhagen. And then, of course, there is Jorn Utzon who designed the Sydney Opera House. He famously won the international design competition in 1956, aged 38. Sadly his relations with Sydney politicians and planners were not smooth, and he left the project halfway through completion, never to return to Australia. Since the 1990s, a new generation of Danish architects has appeared, for example Nielsen, Nielsen and Nielsen, based in Aarhus, Cubo, and Schmidt, Hammer and Lassen. A notable addition to the Copenhagen

---

14   Field, C. and Field, P., *Scandinavian Design* (Copenhagen: Taschen, 2002).

waterfront is the Architekternes Hus (architecture centre) in Gammeldok, by Nielsen, Nielsen and Nielsen.

Danish design then is the outcome of a number of influences: the 'Democratic Approach', perhaps more correctly the desire to design furniture that is stylish, of good quality, practical and affordable; a commitment to and long tradition of supreme craftsmanship, passed from generation to generation; and, in architecture, for the most part a strong appreciation of and sensibility to place, vernacular and human scale. Today, Danish design is known the world over, amongst those who appreciate such things, for classical beauty, elegant simple lines and modern functionality. Less well-known than the Bauhaus, the Danish schools of design have nevertheless survived the test of time and continue to produce new work of rare beauty.

Today Copenhagen has a highly diverse and varied economy.[15] As well as services, the economy still benefits from exports of high value goods and the growth of new industries such as life science, bio-medicine and pharmaceuticals and R&D. The entire Oresund Region is being jointly promoted with Sweden as 'Medicon Valley'. Copenhagen also boasts the largest IT-cluster in Scandinavia with nearly 100,000 employees and is home to Nokia's largest research centre outside Finland. Several international companies have established their regional headquarters in Copenhagen, notably Microsoft. The port still thrives and the world's largest container shipping company has their world headquarters in Copenhagen.[16] This is a story of a rare phenomenon, a creative milieu that still innovates and earns export dollars. Indeed, in design and other media, a good proportion of the city's prosperity is based on artistic activity, although the city's economy is prosperous because of its diversity.

Industry Clusters: The Third Italy and Damietta

Much international interest in small and medium enterprise clusters has followed the success of the 'Third Italy'. From the 1970s, it became apparent that economic progress was fitful in the poor south (Second Italy), despite large-scale regional industrial policy for the Mezzogiorno; while in the traditionally rich northwest (First Italy) traditional industries were stagnating. By contrast, the northeast and centre of Italy experienced impressive growth in a number of sectors where small firms predominated. Groups of firms clustered together in specific regions – Capri and Prato for textiles, Arzignano for leather, Sassuolo for ceramics and Manzano for furniture – seemed to be able to grow rapidly, develop niches in export markets and offer new employment opportunities.

---

15   Andersen, T. M., *The Danish Economy: An International Perspective* (Copenhagen: DJOF Publishing, 2001).

16   Hansen, A. L. and Andersen, H. T., 'Creative Copenhagen: Globalisation, Urban Governance and Social Change', *European Planning Studies*, 9(7), 2001.

Italy achieved a surprising share of world exports for many industrial commodities during the 1970s and 1980s – men's suits, wooden chairs, knitwear, shoes, handbags, ceramic tiles. Most of these are produced in the small firm industrial districts. Sassuolo, for example, is a world centre for ceramic tiles. Prato, near Florence, has 14,000 clothing firms, which together produce 25 per cent of the world's men's suiting cloth. Carpi produces one quarter of Italy's exports of woollen clothing.

These industry networks have strong network of public and private institutions – a largely invisible entrepreneurial infrastructure – which enables them to collaborate in such matters as marketing and R&D. The social context in which this takes place is of great importance, with informal family and social networks often providing a solid and reliable framework for business transactions.[17] The Emilian government, from the late 1970s, played a central role in the growth of the region's economy. It has supplied a wide range of support and finance to the small and medium sized enterprises on which the economy is based. It encouraged export consortia, common service organisations, technology centres, data banks, sectoral market intelligence, computer-aided design systems, training programmes and craft colleges, the underwriting of financial cooperatives and the representation of regional interests at the national level.

Emilia Romagna today is one of the richest European regions and the third Italian region by GDP per capital. As well as the clothing, leather and ceramics industries, there is a strong agricultural sector and also high-value automobile, motor and mechanical production (Ferrari, Ducati, Maserati). Agricultural specialisms include cereals, potatoes, maize, tomatoes and onions, as well as fruit, grapes and wine production, ham and cheese. Food processing is particularly concentrated in Parma, Modena and Bologna. The regional economy is more geared to export markets than other regions of Italy: the main exports are from mechanical engineering, the extraction of non-metallic minerals, and the clothing industry.[18] The region's economy is diverse, varied and complex. It is based around a half a dozen or so small cities.

In this way, the rapid growth of the Third Italy was associated with the concentration of firms in particular sectors and localities. These clusters were able to establish a strong position in world markets in products such as shoes, leather handbags, knitwear, furniture, tiles, musical instruments and food processing. These clusters, crucially, have the capacity to innovate, using technology to adapt production and design processes. Importantly, the 'artisan' firms have

---

17   Brusco, Sebastiano, 'The Emilian Model: Productive Decentralisation and Social Integration', *Cambridge Journal of Economics*, 6, 1982, 167–84.

18   Sforzi, Fabio, 'The Geography of Industrial Districts in Italy', in Goodman, E. and Bamford, J. (eds), *Small Firms and Industrial Districts in Italy* (London: Routledge, 1989), pp. 153–73.

legal exemption from labour and other welfare provisions.[19] By these and other measures, coupled with the area's long-standing traditions of weaving, tailoring and entrepreneurship, the Third Italy has gone from strength to strength, even against a backdrop of sluggish economic growth in Italy and increased competition from China.

The Third Italy is thus an 'industrial district' on a regional scale, that is a series of agglomerations of small firms. These are characterised by the close geographical proximity of the firms themselves, sectoral specialisation, close inter-firm collaboration, inter-firm competition, innovation in design and production, a socio-cultural identity based on trust, and a supportive regional and municipal government. Much the same elements can be found in Damietta.

Damietta is a port town located at a branch of the River Nile near the Mediterranean Sea. The city has a long history and over time has undergone numerous name changes. Damietta is known for its furniture making, tanneries, textile making, confectionery and dairy production, and rice milling. Damietta is also home to one of the largest fishing fleets on the Mediterranean, in addition to a busy port. More recently, Damietta has become a popular destination for tourists.

The furniture cluster in Damietta started as a collection of small, specialised workshops.[20] It has grown over time in size and number of firms to incorporate 75 per cent of the total furniture production in Egypt, generating annual revenue of approximately $100 million. Furniture making employs the largest portion of Damietta's population. Damietta has a reputation in Egypt as being an entrepreneurial community with little or no history of government intervention.

Towards the end of the 1990s the cluster began to experience a number of serious problems relating to product quality, diminishing markets, and aggressive global competition. During the 1970s and 1980s skilled craftsmen began to leave the area in droves to move to Syria and Lebanon. In response, a Committee for Upgrading the Furniture Sector (CUFS) was created through a Decree by the Governor, which included as members representatives from industry and government. The mandate for CUFS was to identify and prioritise problems, develop action plans, enhance collaboration among the 'cluster stakeholders', and 'mobilise' resources. The ultimate goal for CUFS was to help found a non-government organisation that would 'develop operating guidelines and devise task forces' charged with specific tasks to support the 'new catalyst organisation industry development strategy'. The Committee formally registered the Association for Upgrading the Furniture Sector in Damietta (AUFSD). Financial support for the AUFSD was secured through membership fees, members' contributions, and other sources.

AUFSD's programmes to date include an internship scheme, a manufacturers' service centre, international representation of the cluster in international trade

---

19   Murray, F., 'Flexible Specialisation in the "Third Italy"', *Capital & Class, 11(3)*, Winter 1987, 84–95.

20   Parto, Saeed, 'Innovation and Economic Activity: An Institutional Analysis of the Role of Clusters in Industrializing Economies', *Journal of Economic Issues*, 42, 2008.

fairs, the establishment of a database, promoting the establishment of a Faculty of Applied Arts in Damietta, and assistance to 700 factories in production management, skills and equipment upgrading, and marketing. The programme has provided training courses in France and Spain and organised exhibitions for the cluster's products at international fairs such as the Index in Dubai and *Salon de Meubles* in France. AUFSD has managed to secure land, infrastructure and loan facilities from the governorate, and funding and in-kind contributions from international donors for technology procurement and equipment purchases.

The Damietta furniture-making cluster is now regarded as an example of real economic development across the Middle East and beyond. Even so, some problems remain. Tariffs on materials and inputs used in furniture production are unreasonably high while the taxation system provides various barriers for micro enterprises that wish to expand operations. A taxation system favouring exporting firms is being mooted. Damietta's success is, like the Third Italy, based on networked entrepreneurial firms operating as a dynamic cluster.

Boomtowns

Wealth creation flourishes where societies adopt capitalism and Western-style democracy. Take the example of India. Indian cities such as Mumbai and Bangalore are enjoying unprecedented wealth creation, as they benefit from and in part lead the new wave of capitalist economic growth. This is making remarkable inroads into reducing poverty and providing opportunities for economic betterment.

India has been a democracy since 1947, but its early years as a sovereign state – closely allied with the Soviet Union – were characterised by regulation and central planning. The government invested directly in large-scale industrial enterprises and protected them by erecting strong barriers to imports. Businesses could only be set up with permits from the state, after which time the businesses themselves were protected from foreign competition. Economic growth stalled and the proportion of people living below the poverty line increased from 50 per cent in 1947 to 62 per cent in 1966.[21]

Like China, India set about a process of gradual economic reform, but in this case from the mid 1970s. The permit system was wound back, tariffs were reduced and, partly as a consequence, exports increased. Economic growth since the mid 1990s has proceeded at some 10 per cent per annum. This has been led by the southern states of Andhra Pradesh, Karnataka and Tamil Nadu, and the overseas investment they have attracted. This is particularly true of Bangalore where Microsoft opened its first fully-fledged development centre outside the United States. The fact that most Indians can speak English has helped turn cities like Bangalore, Hyderabad and Gurgaon into 'the back office of the world'.

---

21 Norberg, J., *In Defense of Global Capitalism* (Washington, DC: Cato Institute, 2003), p. 51.

One of India's biggest exporting sectors is IT, with companies like Infosys, Wipro and others exporting to the United States. Bangalore, once primarily a resort, has become the centre of India's high-tech, computer-oriented information technology industry.[22] IT giants like Microsoft, Intel, IBM and 3M have all opened production facilities there. The story of Bangalore's emergence as a high-tech industrial centre dates from the 1960s when the Indian government located its defence and research centre in the city. By the 1990s Bangalore was attracting investment from overseas multinationals, and this would be followed by growth of indigenous businesses. India's IT sector now employs 1.3 million people directly plus another three million indirectly, and 40 per cent of this employment is based in Bangalore. New science parks and campuses have been established around the edge of the city: the International Tech Park, Electronic City and Knowledge City. The city now has the highest average income in India.

This phenomenal growth has been accompanied, unsurprisingly, by a rapid increase in population: in 1970 the population of Bangalore was 1.6 million, by 1990 this had increased to 2.8 million and by 2005 it was some 6.5 million. It is projected to reach 10 million by 2015. Because of the increase in population and average incomes, local consumer demand can now support a service economy that was undreamed of just 20 years ago. Some 500 new bars and cafés have sprouted in the city centre alone; the city's young women are becoming increasingly fashion-conscious and there have been several property booms. All of this has not been entirely plain sailing. Rents and housing costs have increased dramatically, but government has failed to invest adequately in public transport or even electricity stations, and the international airport is now struggling to cope. There are also voices arguing that the city is losing its cultural identity, so great is the influx of migrant workers from around India and beyond.

The parallels with this and previous long waves of wealth creation are striking. New industries are taking hold in particular places, so that the early pioneering cities are very often those who succeed the most in economic development and wealth creation. It is this phenomenon that gives rise to episodic periods of spectacular growth and city development. This explains why most cities tend to develop in periodic spurts. This is what is now occurring in India.

Death of a City

The alternative to this growth scenario is one of low growth and welfare dependency, as was the case in India and China before economic reform. In developed Western economies, once dynamic cities can stagnate and decline, for example Glasgow or Pittsburgh. Stagnating and declining cities tend to have very few flexibly-specialised industry sectors, and will often be dominated by large

---

22   Cashin, Paul and Sahay, Ratna, 'Regional Economic Growth and Convergence in India', *Finance and Development*, March, 1996, 49–52.

branch-plant businesses (albeit with more localised supply chains) and a higher proportion of service businesses serving predominantly local consumer demand. Crucially, they lack economic dynamism.

The long slow decline of Adelaide as a city is a lesson to all city leaders who think they can rest on their laurels. History has it that Col. William Light, soldier, explorer and surveyor, established the location for the City of Adelaide in 1836. Light chose an inland site on either side of the Torrens River, with a port at Glenelg and later Port Adelaide. The city itself was laid out in a grid set over 1 square mile. The city was bounded by four 'Terraces' overlooking a ring of parkland, the internal layout organised around five north–south streets, six east–west streets and five city gardens. The grandest streets were 33 yards wide, most of the others 22 yards, and a secondary network of alleyways at 11 yards or half a chain. Over the Torrens lies North Adelaide, also set out on grid but at a 45-degree angle. Here one can find Colonel Light's Lookout and a statue of Adelaide's founder.

Light's status as founder of the city is 'contested' by the urban left, who argue that the site had not been found by Light, Light only managed the survey, and all he did was ratify the plans. The real work was carried out by George Strickland Kingston, a civil engineer and architect based in London.[23] This is held to prove that Light was simply a political appointment and that there has been a conspiracy of silence ever since.[24] Why this 'debate' is not essentially trivial escapes me. In any event, the upshot was that Adelaide was the only Australian city built as a free settlement at the time, that is it was not a penal colony. Building lots were sold to individuals already in Australia, but many people emigrated from the UK to build homes and businesses and start a new life. The city was named after King William's consort.

Adelaide grew rapidly during the mid nineteenth century as a centre of trade, exporting grains, livestock and minerals (opals) from the interior; it was also the administrative centre for South Australia and the Northern Territory, joined to Darwin in the far north by a railway line that crosses the great interior. In the 1870s, Adelaide was the fastest growing city in the British Empire, but this ended with the property crash of the 1880s.

Adelaide's growth from that time was more measured. It became a manufacturing centre in the 1950s and 1960s, notably in engineering and the motor industry. The state's Premier in the 1950s, Sir Thomas Playford, is credited with securing new investment in these industries and with early planning for growth, at Elizabeth New Town. He also commissioned the Metropolitan Plan of 1962.[25] By this time, Adelaide's population was 600,000, and was projected to grow at 3 per cent per annum over 30 years. The Plan's prescriptions were gradually abandoned

23 Langmead, D. and Johnson, D. L., *City of Adelaide Plan: Fiction and Fact*, (Adelaide: Wakefield Press, 1986).

24 Bowe, Chris, 'The Light Myth', *Adelaide Review*, July 2004.

25 Hutchings, A., 'Consistent Vision: The Planning of Metropolitan Adelaide', in Freestone, R. (ed.), *Spirited Cities* (Sydney: The Federation Press, 1983).

during the 1970s and 1980s as, despite an influx of '10 Pound Poms', projected growth failed to materialise.

Adelaide's nadir came with the State Bank collapse of the early 1990s. Caught up in the property bubble of the late 1980s (just like in the 1870s) the State Bank made a series of unwise loans in property and regeneration schemes for the East End in particular. The bank collapse affected thousands of people, led to a collapse in investment in the city and blighted the East End (although this turned out to be a blessing). The state government had its three-star credit rating removed. By this time, of course, the traditional industries on which Adelaide's post-war prosperity had been built were suffering falling profitability and began to shrink. Adelaide was now in serious economic decline.

The response to this was to seek to attract footloose industries to locate in Adelaide, but very few did so. Some took the money, set up shop, stayed for a few years and left again. Meanwhile, those with aspirations to follow a professional or creative career were leaving for Melbourne and Sydney in ever-greater numbers. Adelaide's population began to stagnate and then decline. Government assistance to the car industry became a feature of Adelaide life.

There seemed to be a brief period in the late 1990s when the property market recovered, and when the government of the day invested in a few infrastructure projects. There was also a brief experiment with the arts and creative industries as an economic driver, under the Lord Mayor of the time, Dr Jane Lomax-Smith. However, it was clear that by about 2007, Adelaide was not prospering to anything like the same degree as other Australian cities, and especially Perth and Brisbane.

Adelaide's problem is that no one wants to move there, except a new class of poor refugees. The city continues to lose its young people, the brightest and best, for the simple reason that the economy lacks dynamism and hence opportunity. Some South Australians return from Melbourne or overseas to start a family, but the city's population remains stagnant. Rather than 3 per cent per annum, the much-vaunted population target is now a 15,000 increase, about 1 per cent in total over 15 years. Adelaide's population profile is ageing rapidly.

Now it could be that, in fairness, Adelaide's economic decline was unforeseeable and that there was nothing that anyone could do to overcome it. If this is true, then Adelaide might as well close down now. The other view is that the city, in addition to its economic misfortunes, has been blighted by bad political leadership. This is a familiar refrain in Adelaide as politicians from the city and the state government routinely blame each other, promise to work together but don't, and fail to make wise decisions about the future. This situation has worsened since 2001 and the election of a government whose economic policy centres on uranium mining, but has very little interest in other sectors of the economy or, indeed, in growing new small businesses. Nothing can grow in Adelaide because there is no economic husbandry.

As Jacobs argues in *The Economy of Cities*[26] the primary conflict in city economic development is not between competing existing businesses, nor between labour and capital as economic classes as the Marxists would have us believe. Rather the important conflict is between 'people whose interests are with already crystallised economic activities, and those whose interests are with the emergence of new economic activities'. Where established interests predominate – as in the guilds of medieval London or the Scottish burghs – to the detriment of the new, then only economic stagnation can follow. Where new activities come to predominate, economic growth will result. In circumstances were new growth is a possibility, the role of city and state governments is not to defend the old against the new, or simply to remain neutral, but is to actively promote new forms of economic growth. Otherwise cities will lapse 'into stagnation for the benefit of people who have already become powerful'.[27] This is true of Adelaide, a city no longer but a dormitory town, over-governed and badly managed.

Prague: The Velvet Revolution

During the Dark Ages and early medieval times Prague was seat of the dukes and kings of Bohemia, and a bishopric and archbishopric (from 1344). During this time, the city's main trade was as a slave market. The city flourished during the fourteenth-century reign of Charles IV, King of Bohemia, who also happened to be the Holy Roman Emperor. Charles ordered the building of the Nové Město or New Town, adjacent to the Old Town. The Charles Bridge was erected to connect the new district to Malá Strana. Most of the parts of Prague that charm visitors were built during this time, including the Saint Vitus Cathedral and the Charles University, the oldest in Central Europe. Prague was then the third-largest city in Europe, home to German and Italian merchants, as well as bankers, many of them Jewish. It was one of the first cities to have its own mint. Prague's wealth was based on mercantile capitalism and trade with Italian and German cities.[28]

However, from the early fifteenth century, Prague's political and religious life was turbulent, and this undermined the city's economy. In the early fifteenth century there were attempts by the Hussites to reform the Church, leading to religious conflict, defrenestrations and civil war. Two hundred years later, there followed the Thirty Years' War, crushing defeats to the Swedes, the execution of 27 Czech lords and the exiling of many more. Both the Saxon War and the Swedish occupation took a toll on Prague. The city's population actually declined from 60,000 to 20,000, although this recovered during the second half of the seventeenth century. The great fire of 1689 led to a rebuilding of the city.

---

26 Jacobs, J., *The Economy of Cities* (London: Jonathan Cape, 1969), p. 249.
27 Ibid., p. 250.
28 Burton, R., *Prague: A Cultural and Literary History* (Oxford: Signal Books, 2003).

Prague experienced a period of strong wealth creation through the eighteenth century, and by 1771 had 80,000 inhabitants. Many were rich merchants who built palaces, churches and gardens in the Baroque style. During the industrial revolution factories developed, powered and supplied by the coal mines and ironworks of the surrounding region. By 1837, the population exceeded 100,000.

The First World War ended with the defeat of the Austro-Hungarian Empire and the creation of Czechoslovakia. Prague was chosen as its capital and Prague Castle as the seat of president. Prague was by this time a flourishing economy with a diverse industrial base, strong particularly in car manufacturing and electronics, and also in film production. By 1930, the population had risen to 850,000. But the city's prosperity was reduced by the German invasion of 1939, the Second World War, the Red Army occupation and Communism. Prague was effectively controlled by the Soviet Union, despite having its own Communist Party government. What had been one of the strongest economies of central Europe became stagnated and declined over the next 50 years.

The 4th Czechoslovakian Writers' Congress held in the city in 1967 took a strong position against the regime. President Alexander Dubcek proclaimed 'socialism with a human face', the democratic reform of institutions and everyday life known as 'the Prague Spring'. The Soviet Union and its allies reacted with the invasion of Czechoslovakia and Prague itself in 1968. During this time, writers such as Milan Kundera played a pivotal role in resisting Communism and reigniting interest in Czech literature (and theatre) – for a time in the nineteenth century Prague was a renowned centre for theatre and opera.

Czechoslovakia eventually achieved independence from Communism in 1989.[29] There was very little violence and so the Czechs came to refer to theirs as the Velvet Revolution. Their first democratic president in over 60 years was a playwright, a matter of much pride in the early 1990s. In 1993, after the split of Czechoslovakia, Prague became the capital city of the new Czech Republic.

The arts had played a major role in undermining the Czech Communist state in the eyes of society, through satire and laughter mainly, and during theatre performances in particular. Meanings came to be attached to certain words and phrases, causing audiences to laugh at the irony of it all, but leaving the Russians and Czech Communists none the wiser. Arts venues were therefore places where 'dissidents' could meet and 'talk' in relative safety. Havel himself was able to spread resistance to totalitarianism through allegorical works such as *Redevelopment*,[30] ostensibly a play about town planning and architectural creation:

> As I see it, freedom means not irresponsibility but a final chance to fulfil our creative responsibility. It's primarily a moral question: we must put truth above

---

29   Klaus, V., *Renaissance: The Rebirth of Liberty at the Heart of Europe* (New York: Cato Institute, 1997).

30   Havel, Vaclav, *Redevelopment* (London: Faber and Faber, 1990).

lies, courage above conformity, freedom above repression. To choose pluralism instead of uniformism isn't to choose chaos instead of order, but life instead of death!

An unsung contribution – that is in the West – was that made by jazz venues and the genre itself as a resistance movement to Soviet conformism and the socialist state. The Reduta Jazz Club is located in Narodni, Prague, not far from the National Theatre. The club was opened in 1958, not long after the Hungarian Uprising but 10 years before the Prague Spring. To begin with the music was mainly traditional jazz and swing, big bands and blues, but from the 1960s became increasingly modern. This posed a problem for Communist Party rule, afraid as they were of improvisation and spontaneity. Following the crushing of the Prague Spring, the Jazz Section of the Academy of Arts were arrested, tried and jailed from crimes against the state. Rock bands were banned too. Some of the most influential jazz musicians of the time left for the West, notably Mirloslav Vitous, later a member of Weather Report. For many others this was not an option.

Instead they remained in Prague and for the next 22 years continued to play and even record contemporary jazz in the Reduta and other clubs. Although small, the Reduta became a meeting place for dissidents as well as jazz enthusiasts. Regulars knew each other, and so infiltration by the Secret Police was almost impossible. Under cover of music, people could discuss politics and freedom and how to build a popular resistance to Communism. Jazz was the great musical gift of the United States to the twentieth century, although modern jazz in particular would draw from the work of composers such as Poulenc and Hindemith, Ravel and Debussy. The music of Bud Powell, Charlie Parker, Mingus and Monk was considered too difficult for the untutored ear. In the Soviet bloc, it was considered counter-revolutionary. Fusion, a combination of modern jazz and rock, was considered even more decadent. Of course, this simply encouraged people like Vitous and Jiri Stivin to experiment further in electric jazz.

During the 1970s and 1980s, the Communists cracked down on artists and musicians. Havel himself was arrested several times and made to work as a dustbin collector for the purposes of 're-education'. But, stubbornly, new theatre companies and venues would open up as quickly as they were closed down. An entire generation of Czech actors came through the ranks of organisations such as Studio Ypsilon, a self-organised theatre group. Many went on to careers in film and television. By the late 1980s, artists were openly opposing the dictates and dictat of the state. Dissidents, from being a minority, had become a network of non-violent opposition to totalitarian Communism. Not that this was risk-free, as a sizeable minority within the population supported and worked for the state. Even in the early 1990s, there were many concerned at the possibility of a Communist counter-revolution and seizure of power. Happily this never materialised.

The great thing about the Velvet Revolution is that it was peaceful, but more than this it demonstrated that art and especially jazz can be vehicles for intellectual resistance and freedom. The funny thing is, when it comes to art and improvisation, totalitarian systems of government haven't a clue. Since 1990 Prague's economy has grown steadily. The overall economic structure has shifted more to services, but manufacturing is still strong. Prominent industry sectors include pharmaceuticals, printing, food processing, transport equipment, computer technology and electrical engineering. These provide a strong export base. The city also has strong sectors in financial services, commercial services, trade, restaurants and accommodations. From the late 1980s Prague has become a popular filming location for international productions and Hollywood and Bollywood motion pictures. A combination of the city's architecture, low costs and the pre-existing motion picture infrastructure and studios have proven attractive to international film production companies. Today, Prague is regularly named in businesses surveys as a place of innovation, growth and urban quality. It is now the fifth wealthiest city in Europe, based on GDP per inhabitant, ranking just above Paris.

Prague's story, as told here, is one of a city that had become a self-generating city region economy by the 1920s, only for this to be dashed by war and the Soviet Occupation. However, Prague had the attributes and capability to become a strong and diverse economy once more, and this it has done. Prague has recovered from the man-made disaster that was Communism. The arts – particularly the tradition of theatre and literature – played an important role in the Velvet Revolution, as did the jazz clubs. Even Communism could not eradicate Czech culture. Prague will be one of the cities that will prosper most from the coming period of wealth creation.

Manchester: Cottonopolis to Creative Industry

Manchester is located in the north of England, and jostles with Birmingham as England's second city. Its prosperity was built on the cotton and clothing industries, trading across the British Empire, notably with India, America and Australia (where, interestingly, bed-linen is still referred to as 'Manchester'). Manchester itself became known as 'Cotton-opolis', a status that was only made possible by advanced engineering projects such as the Manchester Ship Canal, extended to Liverpool seaport in 1766. Manchester became the world's first[31] industrial city, triggered to a great degree by Richard Arkwright's patent of a steam-powered cotton manufacturing process, derived from earlier inventions such as Hargreaves's spinning jenny.[32] As well as the new production process, Manchester had access to imported raw materials and markets, plus plentiful local supplies of water and coal. This, plus the fact that Manchester had a repository

---

31   Urban Cultures Ltd and partnerships, *Manchester First: A Cultural Strategy*, available Manchester City Council, Manchester 1992.

32   Hall, P., *Cities in Civilisation* (London: Weidenfeld and Nicolson, 1998), Chapter 10.

of weaving skills following the settlement of Flemish weavers in the fourteenth century,[33] led to cotton becoming the first industrial revolution.

> Manchester: a sky turned coppery by the setting sun; a cloud, strangely shaped resting upon a plain; and under this motionless cover a bristling of chimneys, all tall as obelisks. (Hippolyte Taine)[34]

The rapid expansion of industry led, during the nineteenth century, to rapid urbanisation and conflicts would follow over both working conditions in the mills, and housing and public health: it was in Manchester that Engels would write *The Condition of Working Class in England*. Manchester developed a tradition of trade unionism, the reform of working conditions and social welfare. It also has a strong self-help ethos, particularly in learning and the arts.[35] In the latter half of the nineteenth century, however, Manchester's economic growth slowed and began moving towards decline, largely as a result of competition and a failure to continue innovating. By the middle of the twentieth century the industries that had made Manchester great – cotton, engineering, machine engineering – were largely a thing of the past.

> Little is left of the world in which Manchester built its reputation. The great cotton Mills and warehouses have become converted entertainment venues, the terraced houses models for sets of Coronation Street. What is left, however, is the energy, the sheer spirit that made Manchester one of the great power-houses of the industrial age. And while that age is gone, Manchester is once again picking up steam. (Nicholas Woodsworth, *Financial Times*)

By the 1980s the city's economy was in serious decline, the professionals and middle classes were leaving, the city itself was relatively inert and uninteresting. The city fathers embarked upon a policy of attracting the financial services sector to the city, but this was an uphill task.[36]

However, several interesting things *were* happening. Tony Wilson,[37] an executive at Granada Television and music industry entrepreneur, established Factory Records, a recording label for what would become the Manchester Bands: the Happy Mondays, Joy Division, New Order. Wilson would also open the Hacienda nightclub and Dry Bar, a new generation urban bar. There were

---

33   Girouard, M., *Cities and People* (New Haven: Yale University Press, 1985), Chapter 12.

34   Taine, H., *Notes on England*, translated by E. Hyams (London: Thames and Hudson, 1957).

35   Kennedy, M., *Portrait of Manchester* (Manchester: Robert Hale, 1970).

36   Driver, P., *Manchester Pieces* (London: Picador, 1996), p. 14.

37   Tony Wilson was the founder of Factory Records, and also a TV producer at Granada. The film *24 Hour Party People* is about him.

also the beginnings of regeneration in Castlefield, led by local bookmaker Jim Ramsbottom and a team of young development professionals and architects. As well as the redevelopment itself, this would lead to the emergence of a network of design professionals and architects. The setting up of the Manchester Institute for Popular Culture (MIPC), with a brief to research popular culture, was also important. Amongst other things, an early contribution was a major study of 'The Culture Industry', published in 1990.[38] There was also a timely recognition of the A/V industries (film, television, photography, video) as an important sector, in a study by Comedia in 1988.[39] All of these events were of crucial importance in what was to follow. The problem was that there was no bigger picture in place, no strategy for developing and sustaining creativity. The proof of this is that Factory Records would later go into liquidation, and even the Hacienda was closed.

In November 1991 Manchester City Council commissioned a major study of the arts and cultural policy of the city.[40] The main purpose of the study was to identify the strengths and weaknesses in the city's cultural economy. On the basis of this, the City Council asked the consultants to draw up a strategy aimed at maximising the level and cost-effectiveness of investment in arts and culture; ensuring the accessibility of arts and culture to the city's inhabitants and users; and raising the profile of the city nationally and internationally. As can be seen, the original brief was for a fairly standard arts plan, with the additional goal of raising the city's profile. The consultants opted to challenge and develop this brief to include the cultural industries (production), the cultural economy (consumption and cultural tourism), café culture, the concept of the 24-Hour City, cultural quarters, the public realm, good urban design and architecture.

The strategy took a year to develop, and was a big investment for Manchester at that time. It was entitled *Manchester First*, because it was the first urban cultural strategy of its type in England and Wales, but also because Manchester has always been a pioneering city in theatre, literature, invention and innovation. 'What Manchester does today, London thinks tomorrow'. The document sets a framework for much of Manchester's revitalisation ever since. Other factors were certainly important – the Olympic Bid in 1992, City of Drama in 1994, the IRA bombing the Arndale Centre in 1996, the *24 Hour City* initiative led by the MIPC and Urban Cultures, the redevelopment of the inner-city area of Moss Side. But the cultural strategy formed the basis of Manchester's City Pride Bid, several arts

38   *The Culture Industry*, Manchester Institute for Popular Culture, Manchester 1990. Later re-published by Derek Wynne as *The Culture Industry: The Arts in Urban Regeneration* (Avebury, Aldershot, 1992).

39   *Film, Video and Television: The Audio-visual Economy in the North-west*, December 1988, Comedia Consultancy, for the Independent Film Video and Photography Association, North West Arts, Manchester City Council, the British Film Institute, Channel 4 and Lancashire County Council

40   Urban Cultures Ltd and partnerships, *Manchester First: A Cultural Strategy*, available Manchester City Council, Manchester 1992.

lottery projects, the relaxation of licensing laws, the explosion of café culture and the overall drive towards mixed use and the creation of distinctive quarters.

In this way, Manchester endured a long period of economic decline culminating in a slump, but followed by a unique burst of creativity. Reservoirs of creative talent based on traditional skills, cultural innovation and the presence of three major universities in the city were essential to the early growth of the creative economy, as was the emergence of a new breed of locally-based entrepreneurs. The availability of inexpensive property, brought about by suburbanisation and disinvestment from the urban core, as the middle classes fled the city, allowed new businesses to co-locate in previously unfashionable areas. This in itself helped in the emergence of a network of local design professionals. The backdrop against which all of this occurred included a successful Manchester popular music scene in the 1980s, as well as a reputation for excellence in television production and a longer tradition of theatre and writing.

The emergence of a 'creative class' in Manchester in the late 1980s is probably in part a consequence of events of up to 30 years earlier (particularly in relation to popular music, fashion and arts education). For without the presence of such people in Manchester in the early 1990s, the cultural strategy could not have succeeded. The immediately preceding age of cultural creativity was in the 1970s and 1980s, with the emergence of the Manchester Bands. This was in essence a fusion of popular music and fashion in Manchester in the 1980s. The Manchester of the 1980s was also beginning to innovate in television production – the expertise to do so having been built up by Granada Television (where Tony Wilson started as a trainee) and, to a lesser extent, BBC North West. Piccadilly Radio, one of the first commercial radio stations, blended production with 'Manchester Music' and advertising. Thus the convergence of popular music, fashion, film and television productions (and eventually digital art) was made possible. In addition, historical traditions of live music (the Halle Orchestra and the Northern Conservatorium) and theatre (a pool of actors, stage directors and technicians) and literature (scriptwriters) played their part, as did a steady supply of fine art students, photographers and commercial artists. These were the enabling factors and influences but the creative spark – or trigger – was Tony Wilson with Factory Records, the Hacienda, Dry Bar and Granada Television.

Today, places such as Ancoats, Castlefield, Manchester Northern Quarter and Piccadilly are centres for the creative industries and the arts. Major investment in new facilities has been undertaken, both by the BBC and Granada, and many managed workspaces and conversions now house thousands of small arts and creative businesses. This has been matched by increased investment in cultural facilities and arts venues, such as the Lowry Museum and a cluster of venues at Salford Quays. The Creative Industries and Digital Media sector in Greater Manchester employs around 53,000 people with more than 7,000 businesses. This sector is forecast to grow by 19 per cent during the next decade. Most recently, it has been argued that Manchester's creative sector holds the key to realising the city's ambitions of becoming an internationally renowned city of innovation.[41] Manchester is now the UK's largest 'creative hub' outside London. In a wide range of sectors from TV to software and from advertising to radio, Manchester has more creative businesses than all other northern cities put together. The creative industries now account for 6 per cent of all jobs in Manchester.

Manchester's aspiration, set out by its civic leaders, was to be an internationally renowned city of innovation. To achieve this, the city had to become a place of ideas and creativity, where it was once a home to cotton mills and warehouses. It has succeeded to a good extent by developing its creative industries, in sectors from computer games and software to radio, television and advertising. These businesses are, moreover, a source of innovation for the whole of the economy. However, the city still has serious problems of unemployment and joblessness to overcome. Manchester is indeed known internationally as a city of creative industry, although it also now has a healthier, more diverse economy, including financial services and retailing. But its new way of 'finding a livelihood' is based in good part on creative enterprise.

Commentary

The key point of this discussion of city and city-regional economies is that wealth creation occurs in real places. It is driven by innovation, adaptation, the creative use of technology, entrepreneurship and trade. Cities that develop specialisms thrive, but they must also grow as diverse an economy and division of labour as possible. Where this occurs, prosperity follows, and success breeds itself. This can be seen in the examples of Chicago and Copenhagen and Bangalore, but also of 'industrial districts' such as Damietta. The magic is so powerful that it can overcome stagnation and decline, even including 50 years of Communism. Cities can also bounce back from severe economic restructuring as in the case of Chicago and Manchester. The message seems to be to develop a specialism or niche, but not to let it become a grave. This can only be avoided by a process of industrial diversification and trade, and by repeated innovation. In some cases, the economy and culture of places becomes closely intertwined, as in Italy for example or in the example of Danish Design. Today, this is important as more cities have developed significant creative industries, as well as IT and communications sectors. These days, good cities are artistic as well as entrepreneurial.

But not all wealth-producing cities become artistic centres, for example Detroit or Pittsburgh, Glasgow or Birmingham in the past, or Singapore and Seoul today. A city's openness to artistic creativity and experimentation is an important determinant of whether creative economies or milieux develop and flourish. It is important to develop a city's 'arts infrastructure', as Manchester and Copenhagen

---

41   NESTA (National Endowment for Science, Technology and the Arts), 'Original Modern: Manchester's Journey to Innovation and Growth', 2009.

have done: the necessary buildings, venues, networks and systems that underpin traditional arts and the new creative and media industries. This is rightly a role for local and regional government, as indeed is the shaping of policy to support industrial development in general. The examples of the Third Italy and Damietta show the sorts of things that can succeed. But care must be taken not to over-reach, stifle creativity and entrepreneurship or be tempted to 'pick winners'. Governments should support industrial development, but not seek to control, micro-manage or over-regulate.

The case studies in this and the previous chapter also show that city economies grow over long waves of development as new technologies and industries come to the fore. Chicago is a good example of this, having had three waves of growth up until the 1990s. Copenhagen likewise grew most successfully during the late nineteenth century and again in the 1960s and 1970s. Prague is setting itself on the road to prosperity by growing specialism industries and by a process of industrial diversification more broadly. This seems to be a feature of mature city economies that achieve self-generating prosperity. In the coming upwave, one would expect many cities to repeat this pattern. Leading industries of the coming period will, as before, operate alongside older industries and economic activity more generally, including consumption of everyday goods – food, wine, clothing – and a range of consumer and producer service industries. But the cities that will prosper most are those where the new leading industries are taking, or have taken, root. Leading industries emerge in certain places for very good reasons, usually to do with previous waves of growth and the build up over time of skills and competencies. Government policy too can help develop new hubs of innovative enterprise, as in Bangalore for example or in Singapore. The leading cities of the upwave will be those that innovate, produce and trade.

Chapter 7
The New Upwave

The world's great age begins anew,
The golden years return ...

Percy Bysshe Shelley, *Hellas*

New Work

In this book I have argued that economic life corresponds broadly to long waves of growth and stagnation. These waves last roughly 50–60 years, and also contain within them smaller peaks and troughs that operate around a nine- and 27-year cycle. There have been four such long waves since the 1780s, the last of which covered the post-war period, that is 1948 to 2002. The fifth long wave, on this reckoning, began around the turn of the century. One question all of this raises is what might happen over the curve of the upswing, that is from 2012 roughly to 2030.

The clues for what might happen can be found in the period of the preceding downswing; that is during the 1970s and 1980s. During this time new technologies were developed, and it is these that gave rise to the ascendant new industries of the new upwave. These new industries are based on the Internet, mobile communications and digitisation, and also bio-technology and environmental sciences; the key inventions of the period were computer software, the Internet, digital coding and decoding, DNA and energy saving, solar technology and water-recycling plants.

The underpinning of the upwave – of any upwave – thus lies in the development of new technologies, industries and forms of production, in addition to expanded trade links and developing markets. Already we can see that, because of this, the geography of production is changing with more industrialised goods being manufactured in lower-wage economies. Producer and consumer services are likewise becoming more complex and sophisticated, organised by trendsetters, often as not on websites and blogs.

In this way, the new upwave comprises some economic activities brought forward from earlier waves (industrial production in China, cars, ships, aircraft) plus flexible specialisation for example in clothing and ceramics); the knowledge economy more generally and the media industries; environmental and biological science and marine biology, nano-technology and health technology overall; while consumption of consumer goods and locally-based services and 'experiences' will also rise. Commodities such as grains, wool and cotton will also be required to feed and clothe us. Resources such as oil, iron, coal, copper, rare earths magnesium and zinc will be mined to provide energy, but also the building blocks of new technological products.

Many industries will thus continue to rely on traditional skills married with new technology. Others will develop and diversify into particular brands and specialism, say in food processing or wine. There will be increasing numbers of wealthier and more sophisticated customers seeking 'something different', especially things that one can wear or exhibit in one's home or office. Demand for the plastic arts, designed objects, architecture, interior design, contemporary crafts and fashion will increase. The digital age will continue for many years to follow, creating demand for media content, sights and sounds and games. There will be more industrial production of objects, works and style, through bespoke making and small-batch production. Environmental concerns will continue to be a theme within the more mature economies, but people will come to realise that only societies that are prosperous can afford to protect, renew and re-create natural environments on a sustained basis. Only wealthy societies can pay for pollution-free engines and generators. In the absence of any serious contribution to energy production from renewable sources such as wind farms and solar panels, there will be a need for nuclear power and, if feasible, clean coal technology.

In the early 1990s, Charles Handy[1] caused a stir by pointing towards the knowledge economy and the rise of the portfolio lifestyle where people would have more than one career over the course of their lives. Like firms in the knowledge economy, we would all become more flexibly specialised and be able to earn varying amounts of money at different times in our careers and working lives. People would thus be able to avoid the fate of working for one employer for 45 years. Unfortunately, the recession of 1993 was just around the corner, and many who had taken up the portfolio lifestyle found themselves in financial difficulty and without a regular source of income. This is not quite so serious a problem when the economy is booming, provided people set money aside for leaner times, as I argue later in this chapter.

But it also now seems the case that, beyond the opportunity or fate that is the portfolio career, the nature of work is changing more profoundly. Put simply, the Internet and the easy access to information it provides is destroying as well as creating jobs. For if you can find some information on economic development in Finland by going online, then why pay a consultant to provide you with a report? If you need to know about successful city planning in Copenhagen, you need only click on a website or two. Rather than pay a PR consultant to send out a press release for you, why not simply send out an email newsletter yourself? This means that a good proportion of jobs currently done by consultants and the semi-retired over the age of 50 will simply disappear, and indeed this is already happening. For a good proportion of people, vanishing jobs will be a feature of the next decade and more.

---

1   Handy, C., *The Age of Unreason* (London: Century Business, 1990).

Meaningful employment in middle-class activities such as consultancy, research, urban planning and financial planing will diminish proportionately and perhaps in actuality. The safe careers will be in health, education, government and local government, and probably accountancy (although not if simplified tax regimes are introduced). The elite professions – doctors, lawyers, surveyors – will continue to thrive, but competition for places at good universities will increase significantly. Scientist and technicians should also continue to be in demand. But middle class white-collar jobs are disappearing, as sources of office-bound, paper-pushing activity dry up. Jobs, and the preparation of students for them, should thus be the central concern of educators and policy-makers.

In a sense, the disappearance of middle-class jobs into cyberspace is simply another version of manufacturing jobs being relocated overseas to lower employment cost countries. It is another form of flexible specialisation and the core-periphery employment model. This is true even of retailing, for why buy your books from an expensive store when it is cheaper and easier to use Amazon? Why buy a CD when you can download music for free? Why use a local store at all when you can order direct from the supplier? This implies that in already developed economies rather more of us will work in the service sectors, while some will prosper as middlemen linking economic entities in China or India to consumers in the West. Many will find their jobs have vanished unless they can secure a post in government or a university.

Most of the new jobs that will be created in the coming boom will most probably be in the service sector – waiters, stylists, tour operators, wine suppliers – and the risky path of self-employment and small businesses. But there will also be numbers of highly paid staff, those who are central to the core business of employers – designers, technicians, R&D. On the other hand, rising demand for art and beautiful objects should see an increase in demand for people who work with their hands – ceramicists, weavers, woodworkers, metalsmiths, jewellers. And where would we all be without plumbers, electricians and plasterers? This suggests that one source of new jobs will be in the traditional trades, and for this reason technical colleges and polytechnics should in my view be separated off from the more academic universities once more. Concrete manual skills should be an important aspect of the new economy of the golden age.

In the coming golden age, economies will continue to grow through trade, importing and exporting, increasing local consumption and by twin processes of innovation and diversification. This is what they have always done. All of this will impact on the everyday lives of all of us. In the developing world, more people will be lifted out of poverty. In the developed world, more and more of us will enjoy high levels of wealth and sophistication, and will have more choices to make in how to spend and invest and organise our own lives, even if our career paths are less secure than they were 20 or so years ago. In this chapter I consider how these choices might materialise. I also consider how good societies can continue to prosper, and argue that capitalism coupled with liberal democracy is the best model for successful, tolerant and decent countries. Before doing so, let us briefly consider what happens in a recession.

What Happens in a Recession

In a recession, economic behaviour follows a downward spiral. This is painfully clear from the events of 2008–2009 and their aftermath, yet the misery that recessions cause seems all too often forgotten when growth is strong. Central bankers, in worrying excessively over low levels of inflation, seemed quite to forget that growth is much to be preferred over contraction. And so, whilst this will make uncomfortable reading for many people, it is important to understand how recessions build upon themselves.

First off, the aggregate of demand begins to slow and turn down. This happens because markets become saturated and demand for certain products and services is no longer strong. Or, as we have seen, a recession can be orchestrated by governments putting up interest rates in a bid to ward off inflation. The recession of 2008/2009 is a case in point: a downturn was well underway before the collapse of Lehman Brothers, and was caused by interest rate policy in the first instance. As the cost of borrowing rises, consumers spend less and businesses experience slower growth, even stagnation and decline. Whatever triggers the downturn, commodity prices then start to fall. This causes further rounds of contraction. Lenders begin to have difficulty in obtaining repayments and the level of defaulting and bad debt rises. Bankruptcies increase and more people default on loans, many being forced to sell assets and property to clear debt. Businesses and individuals begin to cancel insurance policies, deemed unnecessary or too expensive. In general, people shy away from taking on debt, preferring to do whatever they can to reduce outstanding loans.

Businesses begin to shed staff, small businesses in particular, but larger groups also begin to move production to lower labour cost countries, or simply to close down plants or offices. Or they might just lay-off staff. Many self-respecting people lose their jobs and become reliant on the dole, the *nouveau pauvre* have arrived. Those over the age of 50 might struggle to gain employment ever again. Unions still press for higher wages, especially for those on lower incomes, but jobs disappear ever more quickly. People in jobs try to sit tight, and so the level of vacancies falls. The standard of living and sense of well-being of most people falls too. Property development schemes are put on hold, some abandoned altogether. Construction in urban centres grinds to a halt, no new projects are embarked upon. As businesses fail, there is an over-supply of commercial property and so shops empty and are left boarded up. Cash is hoarded and those with money buy gold instead of saving with the banks or investing on the stock market. Some buildings mysteriously burst into flames, and indeed there is an increase in crime against property, especially theft, fraud and deception. Property prices slow to a halt and begin to fall, casing more people to lose their houses. Interest rates are slashed but there is no immediate impact on growth. Government suffers a fall in tax revenues and has either to cut spending or borrow money. As governments get into debt, confidence in bonds falls. In order to reduce debt, governments print money, leading some time in the near future to inflation. The more severe the recession, the more severe the problem of unemployment becomes, the more unpaid debt piles up. Social disquiet becomes manifest in protest marches, riots and an increase in divorce and suicides due to financial stress.

The worst recessions in living memory occurred in the 1930s and the early 1990s. Both of these followed a stock market collapse. The current recession began to level off in 2009 as bad debt was removed from the banking system. The stimulus packages of that year may have had a marginal impact, but the real issue was returning the banking system to a position of trust. The strong underlying pattern of trade will reassert itself and growth will follow. Growth is already returning in 2010, with the exception of the United States where government spending is far too high, and private investment is too low. Markets will recover left to their own devices as growth in 'the real economy' comes back and confidence returns. As night follows day, at some point the markets will recover. Then the upwave will continue its momentum of growth.

The Upwave Takes Hold

As the upwave gathers steam, patterns of economic growth and wealth creation will become increasingly evident. Some of these we have already seen during the period 2002–2007. It is likely that the coming period will see a rise in commodity prices and stock markets, followed by a period of heightened growth. As the upwave progresses there will be abundant work and rising living standards. Job vacancies will increase and people will feel better off. There will also be price increases and wage rises, and farmers and the mining sectors will prosper. The rate of bankruptcies will fall and business start-ups will increase again. Debt levels will rise again as people take out loans for housing, cars and university fees, but low real interest rates will make borrowing more affordable for a while at least. Credit will grow and banks and other lenders will be very profitable. Government revenue will be easy to collect and come in rapidly, and so governments will thus be able to afford to spend on welfare programmes and projects to improve the environment. Government spending will increase, and so too government employment. Trade union membership and power will also increase.

Culturally, there will be a new era of the *nouveau riche*: fads, fashions, 'lifestyle products' and conspicuous consumption, so that the service sectors will prosper again, especially in the area of personal services such as hairdressing and body spas. People will once again take growth for granted. Planning permission for new developments in urban centres and on the urban periphery will be more difficult to gain. A shortage of commercial floor-space will build up as growth accelerates, and land prices will rise. Property prices will pick up, and then increase rapidly, especially in dynamic growth centres. Rents will increase. Life insurance premiums will fall as more people take out policies, so too private health insurance. There will be a decrease in crime against property, but an increase in violent crime, much of it fuelled by alcohol. Binge drinking and obesity will rise again. Eventually, interest rates will increase to 'eradicate inflation', and the economy will slow again. Governments will quite likely over-spend on welfare programmes and 'infrastructure projects' many of which will become white elephants: airport terminals, ambitious railway networks, bridges to nowhere and shiny new hospitals and schools. Only wise governments will be able to resist over-spending.

Milestones

To help provide some insight into possible staging posts along the upwave (and subsequent downwave) we should briefly revisit some aspects of the theory of the long waves. The capitalist business cycle is really made up of three sets of interlocking cycles. These operate over nine, 27 and 54 years, more or less. This means that there ought to be a major property boom every 27 years or so, a stock market crash every 54 years or so, and likewise a new upwave beginning every 50-odd years. In between times, the nine-year business cycle follows a pattern of 'prosperity, crisis and liquidity', as investors buy, take stock and sell. As prices on the stock market fall and there is usually a mild downturn. Looking back, we can see that downturns and even mild recessions did in fact occur every nine years or so – in 2000, 1991, 1982, 1973, 1964 and 1955. There were also recessions in 1938 and 1930. Looking forward then, we might expect downturns to occur broadly speaking in 2018, 2027 and 2036.

The most dangerous points in the cycle (for social stability as well as economic decline) are following severe stock market collapses that themselves follow a period of secondary but largely illusory prosperity: in 1929 and 1987. Other stock market collapses can occur, but these are unrelated to long wave trends and are caused by specific panics. Examples include the Panic of 1857 as we have seen, the Panic of 1907 set in train by the collapse of the Knickerbocker Trust Company, and the Sub-prime Crisis of 2008/2009.

Carlota Perez has argued[2] that each long wave or 'technological revolution' causes old technologies to be replaced by the new. There follows an early frenzy of investment in new industries led by a new generation of entrepreneurs. She gives the example of the dot.com boom in the late 1990s, following on from new technological applications based on new inventions in the 1970s and 1980s. Perez points out that, in the rush to profit from these new industries, prices of stocks and shares in them are over-bid. This is corrected by a mini 'crash' and stocks fall

---

2   Perez, C., *Technological Revolutions and Finance Capital* (Cheltenham: Edward Elgar, 2002).

back to more realistic levels. At this point, the upward moment of the upwave is stalled, and this Perez refers to as an 'Inflection Point' where new technologies become part of the mainstream economy. This would seem to be the stage we reached following the dot.com bust, that is around 2002 to 2008, the sub-prime crisis notwithstanding. This means we have already witnessed the emergence of new technologies, a feeding frenzy in the digital economy, the resultant crash and the period of new products and services coming into the market: mobile phones, iPods, PCs, the Internet and so on.

According to Perez, there then follows a 'golden age' where rapid and 'coherent' growth ensues, based on further profitable market penetration, market-making and more and more new and/or improved products and services. This phase of the upwave lasts, judging from historical precedents, for some 20 years at which point a process of market maturation sets in and the new products are no longer new and thus offer declining prospects for profitable investment. At this point, financial capital switches once again into property and there is a major property boom as the upwave peaks, as in 1973 for example. If Perez is right, then we are on the cusp of a golden age.

In this way, each long wave[3] can be broken down into six stages lasting roughly nine years:

- Years 1–8: the early phase of steady growth, marked by increased economic activity, stock market gains and greater fluctuations in prices. The upwave is punctuated by a downturn or recession depending on the timing of the nine-year business cycle. Examples: 2000–2009, 1946–1954, 1893–1902.
- Years 9–17: the upwave regains its momentum and the pace of growth quickens. Full employment returns, wages increase and 'inflation' returns. There is a sharp but short recession, after which property prices rise markedly. Examples: 1955–1963, 1902–1911. 2010–2018?
- Years 18–26: economic growth becomes heightened. Prices surge, the stock market booms and property prices escalate. The end of the upswing is reached. Examples: 1912–1920, 1964–1973. 2019-2028?
- Years 27–35: a period of low growth is followed by a 'secondary peak', another property boom and rapid increases in stocks and share prices. This ends with a major stock market collapse. Examples: 1920–1929, 1974–1987. 2040?

---

3   I am assuming here that the start point for each upwave is marked by the emergence of new products and services onto already established markets. Another way of viewing this is to take the low point of the proceeding downwave as the starting point, most recently 1993. In truth, there is some overlap as the new wave begins during the time of the previous wave's decline. Although the technologies on which the current upwave is based first appeared in the 1970s and 1980s, they were not successfully commercialised until the early part of the twenty-first century.

- Years 36–44: a deep recession follows but this is punctuated by another property boom. Inflation is no longer a problem. Examples: 1930–1939 (except in the United States), 1988–1994.
- Years 45–54: once the depth of the recession has been navigated, there is a period of slow recovery and another property boom. This leads into the next upwave. Examples: 1994–2002, 1940–1948.

It should be stressed that this is not an exact science! Many economists will treat such 'projections' as risible, and perhaps they are right. But it is interesting to ponder how these cycles have played out historically and may do so again. It is as well to at least consider the possibility that economies grow in long waves. If it is true we are now entering a 'golden age' then the panic measures of excessive government spending in 2009 can be seen as unnecessary. The good news is that, as in previous waves, governments will get out of gaol as new wealth generates tax income to reduce government debt.

Centres of New Prosperity

Cities and city regions have always been the key engines of economic development, and this will continue. This is because it is in cities primarily that innovation occurs and entrepreneurs try their luck. Cities also provide ready markets for trade in imported goods. In this way, during 2010, Australia is exporting coal and other minerals to China; China makes goods for export to the United States and Europe in particular (but also back to Australia); China's newly prosperous middle classes are also now consumers of locally produced goods and services, but also imports such as Australian wine.

This process is played out mainly in the cities: Shanghai, Beijing, Xiamen, Shenzhen and Hong Kong (without which there would have been no Shenzhen and no Chinese economic miracle). US cities and city regions, meanwhile, continue to innovate and invent new products and services; London and LA lead the media industries; Germany makes excellent cars in Stuttgart; Scandinavians excel at design and mobile communications; France exports food, wine and fashion from Paris, Lyons and Bordeaux; Milan is the capital of wearable high fashion; Bangalore is centre for software design, Mumbai the home of Bollywood. The ascendant city economies during the upwave will be those that compete successfully in the new industries. Like Manchester and Glasgow, Birmingham and Detroit, London and Paris, Los Angeles and San Francisco, Seattle and Bristol, Philadelphia and London (Hertfordshire) in previous waves, the cities of the new economy will long be associated with a particular episode of growth, and particular industries: Seattle and Portland for software and processors, southern California for computer design and the Internet, London and New York for design, Los Angeles for digitalised films, London for television production, Philadelphia for pharmaceuticals, Helsinki and Stockholm for mobile communications, Tokyo for computers and games.

Cities will also continue to exert an influence over their own city regions, so that successful economic entities of the future will be cities plus countryside. Again, this is already true of San Francisco and Seattle, London and Milan. It could also happen in Brisbane and Lisbon. By contrast, cities with low levels of dynamic creativity will experience relative decline. These include places such as Birmingham, Vienna, Madrid, Rome, Dresden, New Orleans and Detroit. Some of these will continue to be seats of government, while others will remain attractive as places to retire to or bring up children. Others will need to take action now to avoid lagging behind.

The basic preconditions for growth are dynamism and innovation, entrepreneurship and creative adaptation. The more diverse a city's economy, the more prosperous it will be. Successful cities will thus need a repository of advanced technological, artistic and craft skills, or else they will need to import and/or educate to provide these. Unless new businesses are more or less continually created and opportunities to pursue creative careers are provided, this will result only in the city becoming a net exporter of skills and entrepreneurs as the brightest and the best leave for greener pastures.

Meanwhile the new capitalist economies of India, China, Brazil and even Russia will prosper. In China capitalism will bring, as it always does, pressure for democratic reform. Countries such as Mexico, Vietnam and Thailand will also grow rapidly. As they grow, so too will they attract more investment. More and more people will be lifted out of poverty as capitalism spreads, yet failed states and corrupt dictatorships will continue to fail because they drive markets away.

In the already affluent countries such as Britain and Australia and the United States, Canada and New Zealand, individuals will have greater opportunities and options to expand their wealth and that of their families than ever before. Provided governments avoid the temptation to over-tax, over-spend and redistribute wealth by taxation. The 'Anglo-sphere' will be very important in the lead it sets for balancing wealth creation, welfare, democracy the rule of law and good governance. The Europeans will also be an example to watch, but they are more prone to *dirigiste* governments and the state knowing best, and there is some uncertainty over the future of the Euro.

Property Booms

If the world economy is indeed entering a golden age of wealth creation, then property booms will be a feature of the next 20–30 years (and beyond). From what we know of previous waves, a scenario along the following lines is possible: growth in property values will return from about 2011, and by 2012 the boom will be obvious. If there is a mild recession or downturn around 2018, this we might expect will be followed by a prolonged period of growth, and a peaking of the upwave. A property crash along the lines of 1973 is likely to occur roughly some time in the late 2020s.

Taking a risky approach, one might be attempted to bet all on these booms and become wealthy from property trading and development. Lots of people have tried this in the past; some have prospered, many have come unstuck. Timing is all-important, but in any event one should only risk what one can afford to lose. It is certainly unwise to treat your home as a moneymaking machine. A strategy of trading up to sell on and downsize is still a good option, but this too depends on timing and having flexibility to wait for the right moment to sell. Second homes seem attractive, but one needs to be very well off to afford one and all the extra costs of insurance, local rates and repairs. Unless you intend to retire or otherwise move to your second home at some future point, there is little real benefit in owning one unless for the purposes of investment. There remains the danger that too many investment homes will be built, causing a fall in values – this indeed has happened in Ireland, 2000–2008.

First-time buyers will struggle to get into the market, especially in fashionable parts of dynamic cities. This has always been the case and always will be. Governments may introduce grants of various descriptions to help with up-front costs, but these simply add impetus to price increases. The truth is that there is no real way around having to save a deposit, get a job and take out a mortgage. While it will be tempting to plunge into the property market as boom conditions take-off, the thing to remember is that all booms have a crash of some sort eventually.

Investments, Savings and Pensions

During a downturn, cash is king and people move from property, stocks and shares and into gold and silver and diamonds. As the upwave returns, the strong temptation will be to move from gold, silver and fixed bonds back into cash deposits, plus stocks and shares. People will tend to sell low-yielding Treasury Bills, Government Securities, fixed interest products, National Savings Accounts and Building Society accounts. Greater returns and interest will be promised elsewhere and in equities in particular. This will be true and many people will prosper from careful investments. This is perfectly reasonable, as new wealth is created by new work financed by investment by others. But at some point the growth projectory will end, perhaps suddenly, and returns will stagnate and perhaps even fall. The trick will be to benefit from stock market gains but not to risk all. It is best to balance investment portfolios, making sure that only capital one can afford to lose is put at risk. Above all, people should avoid investments that promise very high returns as these may well be Ponzi schemes. If it seems too good to be true, it is.

Because banks borrow short and lend long, eventually there will be another run on some banks – this can happen at any time, even in an upwave. It is therefore advisable to distribute cash savings across different accounts so that deposits are guaranteed. In general, the old Chinese system of keeping a third of one's assets in cash, a third in property and a third on the stock market or in bonds has much to recommend it. This provides a hedge against a sudden problem of liquidity, keeps a roof over your head and potentially earns new wealth to re-invest. The main thing is to keep a diverse portfolio of assets, including cash deposits, not to rely on any single investment and ignore get-rich schemes that are usually too good to be true.

One of the recurring questions of our time is whether we can we trust governments to look after pensions and our standard of living in old age. The portents are not encouraging. In the UK, National Insurance was introduced just after the Second World War. This was distinct from general taxation, the public being assured that the monies collected would go into a separate fund to meet future requirements for pensions, unemployment benefit and social security. But no such fund was ever established, so that pensions have to be met from current tax revenues, meaning that increases in pensions have to be balanced against other government expenditures and tax-raising. None of this was helped by the then Chancellor of the Exchequer's, Gordon Brown, decision to raid private pensions in the UK in 1997 and every year since. To cap it all off, some British pensioners are denied upgrades for inflation if they live in Australia, New Zealand, Canada or South Africa, so that the value of their pension decreases alarmingly over a few years.

Governments, then, are adept at changing the rules without notice. Say you have worked out a pension plan based on current expectations of growth and tax incentives ... and then the government arbitrarily removes any tax concessions leaving you with a projected shortfall? In such circumstances, it would be rash to rely on the government for one's only source of income in your retirement.

Australia is better placed with its compulsory private superannuation schemes introduced in the early 1990s. However, much depends at present on the date of retirement and the performance of the stock market at that time. In 2008, many pensioners found that their funds matured just at the time when the stock markets were falling by up to 40 per cent. Some reform to guarantee a minimum amount or to enable more flexibility in when to mature the fund would seem necessary. At the moment, then, super schemes in Australia are not yet sufficiently flexible and they are also over-taxed. Yet the basis of the scheme has much to commend it. In addition, however, one might take out as many other savings plans as can be afforded. A good model was the Tax Exempt Savings Scheme (TESSA) introduced by the John Major government in the UK in the early 1990s.

Health and Education

One of the big questions facing Western governments is the extent they can make good on promises to guarantee entitlements to low cost or free health care and education. This will seem possible as economic growth returns, but 'equal access' health care and education is a movable feast. The costs of meeting any such commitments are very large and will continue to rise, especially in health. As we get older, we need more health care on average. It is prudent to make provision for your own health care if you can afford to do so. Sensible governments would reinstate tax allowances for private health premiums, enabling more people to receive care. In the absence of these, private health premiums will remain too expensive for many, whereas if more people join a given scheme, premiums should fall or at least not go on rising in price inexorably. If you cannot afford private health insurance, then you should have your own savings account set aside for emergencies.

As for education, my advice is to follow the example of left-wing politicians in the UK and United States and other places – Tony Blair, Barack Obama, the Clintons, Diane Abbott, Harriet Harman – by sending your children to a private school. This sets the scene for going on to the better universities later in life. It also obviates the need to have your children exposed to post-modern education 'theory' and government-imposed curricula. Children so educated should have the confidence to read traditional subjects at university, for example literature or the history of art, as well as more vocational subjects such as law and surveying. The other way to achieve this is to move to a town and catchment area for a good state school. It is not surprising that in many counties there are at times heated debates over university tuition fees, since most governments seem to think that half of the population should go to university. This cannot be paid for out of taxation, and so fees must rise. But usually government-backed low cost loans can be taken out, and these can be paid back over a period of many years during which time the level of the debt is eroded by inflation. Setting up an education fees account for your children would seem a good idea. In general, the aim should be to save as much as possible in accounts over which you can exercise control, and do not trust the government to look after you.

Manners

Manners[4] are a set of principles and values that reflect a society's culture and identity. These are set rules governing 'bodily decency and decorum, and forms of dress, address, and demeanour'. Manners are also a way of 'structuring and interpreting the social world', an argument that is also posited by Pierre Bourdieu in his sociological treatise *Taste*.[5] That manners and taste – even patterns of speech – can be used to signal a person's standing in society (including their class) is not at issue, and it is true that some concepts of good manners are more or less

---

4   Bryson, A., *From Courtesy to Civility: Changing Codes of Conduct in Early Modern England* (Oxford: Clarendon Press, 1998).

5   Bourdieu, P., *Taste: A Social Critique of the Judgement of Distinction* (Cambridge, MA: MIT Press, 1984).

a game of social differentiation,[6] taken up these days by aspiring celebrities. Even so, the essential point about manners is that, whilst they evolve as societies themselves change, they nevertheless also have the intended effect of civilising social behaviour.

Robert Beckman[7] argues that cultural characteristics and values reflect consumer mentality, and this is especially noticeable in the final stages of an upswing. He argues that the West rejected previous forms of authority in the late eighteenth century (the American and French revolutions), and in the late mid-nineteenth century (atheism versus the Church). The 1920s witnessed a surge in personal freedom with the development of the self (Freudian psychology) and syncopation (jazz). The late 1950s gave rise to rock and roll and 'the teenager', followed in the 1960s by the 'permissive society'. Beckman argues that 'fashion, music, literature, theatre and dance all fall under the influence of the upwave'.[8] He goes on to propose that women's fashions are closely linked to upwaves and downwaves, particularly in relation to hemlines, necklines, and whether backs are covered or bare. Fashions such as low-cut bodices and accentuated *derrieres* were evident in the fifteenth century, in Elizabethan England and at the time of the Reformation (1660). In between times, necklines were higher and hemlines lower. In the most recent upswing we can see the rise of hemlines in the 1950s, the miniskirt in the 1960s, hot pants, glam and punk rock. By the time the downswing had produced evident economic crisis – the early 1980s – fashions were more formal once again.

In this way, social mores also change over the economic cycle. Peaks of permissive behaviour tend to occur during the final years of the upwave and in the period immediately following, for example in the 1960s and 1970s, 1920s and the 1890s and the naughty 1990s. As the rate of profitability and wealth creation declines, behaviour becomes more moderate again and there are often calls for better manners and standards of public decency. This occurred in the 1930s and 1940s, and again in the 1980s and early 1990s.

It is interesting to note that, at the end of the first decade of the twenty-first century, moral codes are making a comeback. Standards of behaviour and decency and appropriate clothing in social situations are being discussed once more. 'Dress Down Friday' is being replaced by suits and proper business attire once more; weather girls on UK television are wearing long below-the-knee skirts again. There are also examples of governments seeking to impose morality on people, notably in the form of sin taxes and bans on smoking. This is a new form of Puritanism, partly driven by health concerns but also reflects the view that governments know best and need to save us all from binge-drinking and obesity.

In the face of this government-sponsored morality, for the next few years, we shall most likely become more serious and circumspect. Students will go to

---

6   Colin Campbell, Lady, *Guide to Being a Modern Lady* (London: Heterodox, 1986).
7   Beckman, R., *The Downwave* (London: Pan Books, 1983).
8   Ibid., p. 42.

university to study professional disciplines again as opposed, say, to gender studies or media studies. People will be scrambling to reduce debt and to get a good job as quickly as possible. Older people will value their local place more and seek out the enjoyment of simple things. There will be less travel overall, especially long-haul flying. People will tend to stay put, including in their places of employment. But this will not last.

As the upwave recovers its momentum we shall most likely witness a time of permissiveness, instant gratification, promiscuity and political extremism. Generally speaking, the final years of upwaves are characterised by increased permissiveness and self-indulgence, such as in the 1960s and 1920s. Women's clothing tends to get more and more revealing, although how this is possible I cannot see. It will be difficult to maintain what are perceived to be old moral values. This portends 'falling standards' of behaviour, public 'indecency', women behaving as badly as men, displays of body parts and a general coarsening of public life. More and more ginger groups and self-appointed 'activists' will clamour for our attention. Of course, thinking people do not have to follow the instincts of the herd, and so there will always be a place for taste, elegance and manners.

Good Societies

The Scottish philosopher Adam Smith wrote in 1775: 'Little else is requisite to carry a state to the highest degree of opulence from the lowest barbarianism but peace, easy taxes, and a tolerable administration of justice.' This seems perfectly true, although during the twentieth century the role of government would extend into areas such as health care, social work and welfare benefits. Since the 1880s the state has been drawn into building infrastructure (or in the case of the railways enabling land purchase) and the direct provision of social services. Historically this was to correct the spread of disease in London, Paris, Berlin, New York and Chicago, and also to provide homes for the urban poor. Hospital services and schools would follow so that by the 1930s Britain at least was well on the road to the Welfare State. The Beveridge Report of 1944 systematised state social welfare in the form of health insurance, pensions, unemployment benefits and social security. These measures undoubtedly addressed the issues of the time (from clean drinking water and a system of underground sewers in the 1880s to the 1947 Education Act), and also contributed to economic growth in the 1950s (through improved health, numeracy and literacy). But since the 1970s, it has become increasingly clear that such programmes cannot be paid for without taxation levels that are too high.[9]

Since at least the eighteenth century successful Western societies have been based on four key concepts or 'pillars' as summarised in Figure 7.1: personal

---

9   Bacon, R. and Eltis, W., *Britain's Economic Problem: Too Few Producers* (London: Macmillan, 1976).

freedom and individual liberty; free market economies; security, stability and freedom from want; and representative democracy. To this extent the secret of the life of good societies is not complicated. The first requirement is peace and justice administered under the rule of law. This is similar to the 'social contract' of Thomas Hobbes[10] where the individual's right to behave as he or she pleases is tempered by respect for law, in return for peace and stability. It was often to pay for protection and security that people were most prepared to pay taxes – to live within the city walls of the medieval city, for example. Stability and security refer in the main to protection from foreign aggressors and from crime, in other words peace and justice administered under the rule of law. Thus standing armies are maintained to defend a country, its citizens and interests; while policing was introduced formally in the nineteenth century to lower the incidence of crime.

The most important attribute of liberal Western democracies is freedom of the individual, including the right to free speech and of association, including religious belief. Put simply, individual freedom means being able to live one's life without undue influence by the monarch or the state or the secret police. Democracy is the system of government that allows for leadership to be changed through the ballot box. This system of governance dates not from the French Revolution nor even the American Constitution of 1776 as is popularly imagined, but rather from the Glorious Revolution of 1688 in England. This provided for ongoing limited government – a sort of pragmatic incrementalism – with checks and balances against the abuse of power, whether by the Monarch or by Parliament. This system was crucially underpinned by individual rights, especially the right to private property. This system of governance provided the backdrop for religious tolerance, universal suffrage and free market capitalism.

Freedom from want implies setting in place a minimum safety net to help fellow citizens temporarily in difficulty. Most Western societies now have safety net social security, dole and subsidised health care systems. It seems likely that governments everywhere will need at some point to move to models of health and pension provision based on investment and private insurance.

Successful societies are based on shared principles, acknowledged truths, respect and tolerance, decency, manners and a set of core values. This includes the tenets of civilised life, including customs and pleasures and also the arts, and the ways and means of conducting public life over the centuries. This is why the study of the humanities is so important and needs to be reclaimed from post-modernism for the sake of joy, erudition and the wisdom of ages. Societies organised around the tenets of representative democracy, stability, individual freedoms, a set of core beliefs and traditions and market economies are the best bulwark against government bullying, tyranny and corruption.

---

10   This notion dates from Plato and Lucretius but its chief exponent was Hobbes who argued that the creation of the state in turn created mutual obligations between the state and the people.

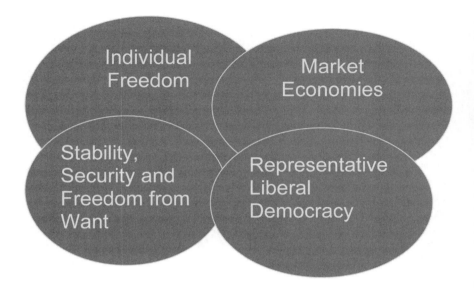

Figure 7.1 A philosophy of society

Commentary

As the upwave progresses, people will start to behave differently, they will be more open to risk as the world is seen as relatively risk-free again. There will be business start-ups, more borrowing to invest in enterprises, property and in improving living standards. All forms of investment – the stock market, property investment, even currency trading – all of these will offer good returns. Trade barriers will be reduced and free trade agreements signed between the more dynamic economies. Some will opt for protectionism, probably the European Union where growth will lag behind the new economies and the Asia-Pacific rim. But overall, the scenario is one of growth and prosperity.

There will be those for whom the new period of wealth creation signals nothing less than vulgarity, greed and materialism, an argument almost as old as the hills. But this misses the point rather, for it is one thing for new wealth to be created by capitalism but quite another as to how individuals and societies choose to behave. Perhaps the real question is to what extent people give to charity, willingly pay sensible levels of taxation for social services and a safety net, and to which people are taken out of poverty in the Third World.

Besides inventing modern economics, Adam Smith was a moral philosopher, indeed that is how he thought of himself. Smith argued that men act in their own self-interest by feeding, clothing and housing themselves and their families; they also act in enlightened self-interest and are able to use 'imaginative sympathy' to understand the feelings and circumstances of others. More than this, good people he argues are able to discern what are good and bad actions and to construct a set of moral principles for living a good life. It is for this purpose that the Rule of Law exists to 'protect the weak, curb the violent and chastise the guilty'. Within ourselves we can live in a state of imperfect virtue, by means of self-command and our behaviour. And this brings us back to an understanding of the self as Kierkegaard[11] would later argue, that is the principle of self-love and choosing to be a good person. We are neither innately good nor evil but can choose to be either. We are not perfect, but we can try, and it is through our actions that our decency or otherwise is manifest.

How can we as individuals make best use of the upwave and its potential for new wealth creation? That depends on the choices we make, but we can only make them if we have the means to do so. There are two broad ways people might respond. For some, most perhaps, the good times will be too tempting. There will be a rise in spending on status symbols, people will become more acquisitive again, they will run up debt, become addicted to technological goods such as iPhones, buy second homes, speculate on the stock market and buy cars once more. That is their choice.

Others will see the increase in wealth as a chance to live the good life, by downsizing, enjoying a more modest but nonetheless comfortable standard of living, find new ways of making a living, leave the cities for small towns and the accessible countryside, and in general terms become more 'green'. The wise people will save more, play the long game, semi but not fully retire, learn to appreciate the simple things in life and build their lives around family, home, friends and work they enjoy. This, of course, is only possible because the general level of income has reached a level where people can afford to do this.

As capitalism creates more wealth, more of us can return to the simple life. This is an irony, but nonetheless true. In this way the downsizers can only really afford their lifestyle if others are working, creating wealth and consuming, especially where their assets are invested in superannuation funds and stocks and shares. Being better off does not make us bad people. Helping others is only a choice if we have first been able to look after ourselves and our families.

---

11   Kierkegaard, Soren, *Either/Or* (London: Penguin, 1992), vol. 1, p. 25.

Chapter 8

Epilogue

We were the first to assert that the more complicated the forms of civilisation,
the more restricted the freedom of the individual must become.

Benito Mussolini

Summary: A Golden Age

Following Joseph Schumpeter, Kondratieff, Robert Beckman and others, I have
argued that capitalism grows in long waves. There have been four of these long
waves since 1780. The fifth wave is underway, having commenced around the
turn of the century. Each wave consists of an upwave of about 30 years, that is a
period of heightened wealth creation punctuated by periodic mild downturns, or
recessions, every nine years or so. The upwave peaks as new technologies reach
the point of market saturation, and investment switches into property. A property
boom and crash is followed by a period of secondary prosperity in the lead up to a
once-in-60-year stock market crash. There follows a period of over-investment in
property, higher inflation and then a deeper than normal recession. Recovery from
the recession is slow to begin with but gathers pace as the next upwave begins.

The waves are caused by new technological advances, their commercialisation
by innovative entrepreneurs, and the creation of new products, services, processes
and markets.

Each wave is, of itself, a period of propulsive growth and wealth creation.
Annual rates of GDP growth vary from 2–15 per cent, depending on a country's
economic 'settings' and attitude to inflation and entrepreneurship. Some countries
grow faster than others, but overall the average wealth in capitalist economies
doubles every 8–15 years during an upwave. This wealth, however, is not produced
in an even spread across the geography of a country but is concentrated in particular
places. These places are city regions such as Milan or London or Shenzhen where
innovation is a way of life and entrepreneurs have access to a gene pool of skills
and aptitudes. Wealth is generated by products and services produced in these city
regions and exported to other places, including other city regions.[1] Thus, without
trade, there can be no economic development. Other regions of countries also
flourish, notably agricultural producing areas and those with large or important
mineral deposits – the raw materials of new wealth: oil, gas, coal, copper, zinc,

---

1   Adam Smith pointed out the importance of domestic trade as well as overseas trade.
Thus, Glasgow trades with Edinburgh and London, as well as New York and Stuttgart.

iron ore, magnesium, aluminium. Lucky countries have deposits of such mineral wealth, and also dynamic wealth-producing city regions.

Governments can either support or hinder this new period of wealth creation. Broadly speaking, governments should choose to support innovation, entrepreneurship and the growth of new industries. This implies policies to promote entrepreneurship and shared intelligence, the eduction and training of highly skilled workforces, support for the proto-type development of new technologies, and regulatory systems that encourage investment and risk as opposed to ever-increasing 'compliance'. Of these, a benign or encouraging regulatory regime is the most important. Entrepreneurs and inventors might welcome some assistance, but even in a time of increased networking and collaboration, inventions and patents must be secured. Invention, like capitalism itself, is often highly competitive. Governments that impose too many compliance procedures and too-high taxes will not succeed economically, or socially, for the simple reason that entrepreneurs, investors and innovators will move to other countries and other states.

Traditional or orthodox economics is a world away from being relevant to – or even understanding – innovation, wealth creation and the key role of city regions. Traditional economists see the world through a prism of over-detailed econometrics gathered and analysed at the level of the nation state (rather than growth regions), and of macroeconomic theories that seek to achieve an economic equilibrium when, by their nature, economic systems are open, dynamic and non-linear. When an economy is in a state of equilibrium, it is stagnant, even dead. Orthodox economics do not, therefore, provide the theories and tools required to grow innovative and propulsive economies.

Even in their own terms – seeking an equilibrium of supply and demand or balancing unemployment against inflation – orthodox economics fail miserably, and often. Abrupt and excessive shifts in interest rates, intended, according to Monetarism, to smooth out peaks and troughs, have instead the effect of making the peaks higher and the troughs deeper. An over-arching fear of inflation leads to growth being cut-off or constrained every couple of years. It would be better to allow banks to set their own interest rates, relieving us of the instability of rapid changes in official policy. To be sure, the swings in interest rate setting since 2001 could hardly have been more extreme, and it is these that helped cause and trigger the sub-prime mortgage crisis. Money was too cheap and then, suddenly, too expensive for the people who had bought the mortgages. The return to Keynesianism in the form of large-scale government spending and borrowing is no improvement on Monetarism, and can already be seen to be profligate, wasteful, poorly targeted and inefficient. This new – or rather old – economic fad will not last long, but its unintended consequences will take time to repair.

New theorisation[2] in the dusty field of economics has argued that economies, as open and dynamic systems, are ecologies rather than mathematical models.

---

2   See Beinhocker, E., *The Origin of Wealth* (London: Random House, 2007) for a good summary.

They are complex because they are dynamic, and dynamic because they are complex. Governments will therefore need a very light and sure-footed touch if their interventions are to be helpful. As Hayek argued 70 years ago, 'human deductive rationality' is simply not up to the task of analysing, predicting and planning economic systems that are open-ended and dynamic.[3] If these new economists are right, then it is important that governments limit their interventions in economies to minimal, sensible levels of regulation and taxation, and to helping provide a growth-oriented business environment. In this latter case, governments can theoretically help 'shape the fitness of the business environment'. This has the advantage of having markets operate effectively, and thus the distribution of outcomes to be as efficient as possible. However, governments will need to beware the likelihood of unintended consequences and the limits of planners' abilities to second-guess markets. The sensible approach is to allow markets to generate prosperity, and use some proportion of the wealth they create for welfare.

But, finally, capitalism will continue to grow along the trajectory of business cycles, upwaves and downwaves, booms and busts. This happened under more or less laissez-faire conditions in the early nineteenth century, and later that same century under Whig Utilitarianism. It happened in the early twentieth century when the economic orthodoxy was neo-classical mathematical modelling, and it happened in the 1950s, 1960s and 1970s under Keynesianism. In 1987–1993 we had a stock market crash and 60-year recession despite the attendant wisdom of Monetarism. Economies grow in such waves because they are natural systems influenced by the behaviour and expectations of humans. Booms and busts are a natural consequence that little can be done to prevent. That is not the same, however, as failing to comprehend the nature of the long waves, nor of being unable to understand where we are in the cycle at any given point in time. An appreciation of this should have enabled policy-makers to understand that 2009 was not another Great Depression.

Although it may not seem like it now (mid 2010), the coming years will see remarkable wealth creation. Because of this, as in previous waves, millions of people will be lifted out of poverty around the world. The new upwave will be the greatest yet episode of wealth creation in human history.

Governments versus Markets?

> The man of system ... is apt to be very wise in his own conceit; and is often so enamored with the supposed beauty of his ideal plan of government, that he cannot suffer the smallest deviation from any part of it ... He seems to imagine that he can arrange the different members of a great society with as much ease as the hand arranges the different pieces upon a chess board. (Adam Smith, *The Theory of Moral Sentiments*)

---

3 Hayek von, F. A., *The Road to Serfdom* (London: George Routledge and Sons, 1944).

Following the sub-prime crisis and the banking panic of 2008/2009 the ideological attack on free market economies has been rejoined. Some on the Left apparently see an opportunity to move towards greater state control of economies and, indeed, everyday life.

> From time to time in human history there occur certain events of truly seismic significance, events that mark a turning point between one epoch and the next, when one orthodoxy is overthrown and another takes its place.[4]

Kevin Rudd, Australia's Prime Minister (until he was deposed on 24 June 2010) calls for a new 'system of open markets, unambiguously regulated by an activist State and one in which the State intervenes to reduce the greater inequalities that markets will inevitably generate'. Rudd believes that governments are better 'determinants' than markets of 'not only efficiency but also equity'. This is a change away from the Centre Left's previous position that acknowledges the need for wealth creation and the role of markets, subject to regulation. Effectively Rudd is arguing for the state to direct more and more economic activity. This is tricky ground, as there is a point where capitalism will cease to be based on free markets if the state abrogates too strong a role to itself. That said, other than a return to Keynesianism and old-style state social democracy, it is difficult to see what this new epoch-shaping orthodoxy might be.

The old New Left is currently arguing that 'Neo-Liberalism' is to blame for the recession of 2008–2009, and yet as we have seen the real causes are more prosaic: interest rate policy, bad debt and derivatives. The case they make is that the removal of regulations has allowed markets to ride roughshod over all before them, a modern return to *laissez-faire*. But this is simply not true. Modern economies are heavily regulated, and government controls about 35–50 per cent of all economic activity in most advanced countries. Indeed, the sub-prime crisis was caused, at root, by government intervention in the housing and mortgage markets and not by 'Neo-Liberalism' at all.

Some commentators are now calling for radical change and an end to market-based economies: the notion that prosperity and economic growth are best achieved by the actions of individuals pursuing their self-interest within freely functioning markets. A good, or rather bad, example is Robert Manne, a professor of politics at La Trobe University, who has rushed to publish a co-edited book *Goodbye to All That? On the Failure of Neo-Liberalism and the Urgency of Change*.[5] Manne is opposed to market-based competition as the basis of economic development and wealth creation: he opposes international trade, but supports monopolies and cartels controlled by the state, he calls for key economic sectors to be nationalised;

---

4   Rudd, K., 'The Global Financial Crisis', *The Monthly*, February 2009.

5   Manne, R. and McKnight, D., *Goodbye to All That? On the Failure of Neo-Liberalism and the Urgency of Change* (Sydney: Black Inc, 2010).

and for 'radical thought and bold imagination' to develop 'non-market ways of addressing social needs'.

Manne has form when it comes to rushing out books into print following an economic recession. In 1992 he published *Shutdown: The Failure of Economic Rationalism and How to Rescue Australia*. In this earlier opus, he argued that Paul Keating's Labor government's economic reforms – tariff reductions, the ending of import protection, privatisation – would lead to 'permanent high unemployment' of 15–20 per cent. Of course, this never happened, and the Australian economy went on to prosper, unemployment rates falling to 4 per cent. Manne proposed a much larger role for government in directing economic development through, for example, 'the rapid building of local factories to produce consumer goods like TVs and VCRs'. Manne clearly does not understand trade and specialisation. Manne's co-editor on *Shutdown*, John Carroll, now writes that '*Shutdown* was basically wrong … if in doubt, trust the free market'.[6]

Manne, of course, is an easy target. Yet he is not alone. Gordon Brown's head of Downing Street Policy Unit, Nick Pearce,[7] argues in favour of a 'more egalitarian and secure market economy, properly regulated and bounded in its sphere' without suggesting what this might be. Meanwhile, in the same journal issue, Pascal Bruckner asserts that Europe, 'home to socialism', has been 'completely conquered' by economics. He argues in favour of a 'single grand project' based on 'an alliance of democracy, science and prosperity' in order to 'liberate the human race'. Europe should, says Bruckner, 'rediscover its fighting spirit'. Some of us would prefer it if it didn't.

Then there is Will Hutton's latest attack on the unfairness of modern capitalism.[8] Hutton tells us that we 'ache' for a 'compelling, moral, national story'. Hutton sets out to define 'fairness' and its role in keeping capitalism on 'its tightrope', but he never quite gets there, other than calling for a greater role for the state in matters economic. To be fair, Hutton explores why the recent 'financial crisis' happened, condemning both Gordon Brown and Alan Greenspan for their regulatory failures. But he is curiously mute on the role of interest rate policy and the role of government in creating the sub-prime problem in the first place.

Finally, Peter Kellner, another veteran left-wing commentator, offers us a new vision for 'social democracy'.[9] Kellner at least admits that there is a problem of government over-spending, noting that since 1952 the economy has grown by 400 per cent but that public spending has grown 1,000 per cent. Most of this has been on the 'three main components of social democracy spending' – health, education and social security. This, notes Kellner, has been paid for by savings

---

6   Carroll, J., 'Economic Consensus Calls for a Bit of Give and Take', *The Australian*, 24–25 April 2010.

7   Pearce, N., 'Measured Progress', *RSA Journal*, Summer 2010, pp. 15–19.

8   Hutton, W., *Them and Us: Politics, Greed and Inequality* (London: Little Brown, 2010).

9   Kellner, P., *The Crisis of Social Democracy* (London: Demos, September 2010).

in other spending areas – such as defence – and by much higher taxation. Kellner concludes that the UK economy is 'at or near the maximum level of overall taxation that the electorate, and Britain's status as an open economy, will bear'. That is, around 46 per cent. Social democracy 'in its familiar form' is 'on the verge' of being unaffordable. Kellner then goes on to propose new ways of paying for social democracy. He might be better setting limits on what can and cannot be afforded by market economies if they are also to prosper and create the necessary wealth to pay for social services.

The Left critics, on this reading, have very little to offer of any practical value. No one seems to know what the 'Third Way' between market economies and State planning looks like. The puzzling thing is that they seem to be overlooking a real-life experiment in 'Third Way' economics. In June 1997, Tony Blair led his New Labour party to victory in the UK general election. Blair promised a Third Way, a blend of capitalism and socialism, also referred to as the 'social market'. This was seen as a breakthrough for the 'Anglosphere', an approach seeking to combine the dynamic markets of the United States and Asia with central planning and state socialism. But it is now clear that New Labour failed, leaving the UK economy in a state of low growth with accumulated government debt. It promised a Panglossian best of all worlds: freedom as well as 'fairness', wealth creation and greater equality, 'low' taxes and high levels of welfare provision. We can see now that these objectives can never be met. A dynamic, competitive economy with a socially mobile society can only succeed where there are incentives and rewards, and thus differing levels of achievement and incomes. This is what Smith called the 'Division of Labour'. If there is no reward for risk and enterprise, there will be no reason to invest or work hard.

Putting taxes up to pay for social programmes, moreover, is fraught with the risk that wealth creation and therefore tax revenues may be choked off or otherwise falter due to wider economic events. As early as 2004, it was clear that government spending in Britain was increasing at a rate that was 'unsustainable': government spending was increasing more rapidly than economic growth and tax income. New Labour's response was to borrow money and, simultaneously, extend state control of the most important functions of national life. This was quite deliberate. Tony Blair's mentor, Anthony Giddens, in his seminal New Labour treatise *The Third Way*, put it like this: 'There will never be a common morality of the citizenship until a majority of the population benefits from the welfare state.'[10] One-third of households in Britain now receive more than half their income in state benefits.

This was accompanied by unprecedented incursions into individual liberties in the form of 'equalities' policing, the reification of multi-culturalism and the end of free speech, much greater use of electronic surveillance, Criminal Background Checks and the promised introduction of identity cards, 'community safety' and a panoply of 'health and safety' procedures and compliance checks. For the Left,

---

10   Giddens, A., *The Third Way. The Renewal of Social Democracy* (Cambridge: Polity, 1998).

who have attempted to undermine the old ways of doing things – family, Church, society, jurisprudence, manners – the new deadly sins are racism, misogyny, homophobia, smoking, obesity, religious belief and climate change 'denial'. These are all thought 'crimes' of an Orwellian tinge.

The New Labour experiment involved a steady increase in taxation and large increases in government spending, to the point where more is spent in benefits than is raised in income tax. The UK government spent an estimated £680 billion during the financial year 2009–2010 on the public sector, running an annual £180 billion deficit. This means the UK government spends £180 billion a year more than it 'earns'. The National Health Service budget, for example, grew by 60 per cent over the period 2001–2009. Spending on health now accounts for £120 billion a year, more than a fifth of all spending. Spending on pensions is also £120 billion, plus £105 billion each on education and social security, and £85 billion on local government. In this way, almost 80 per cent of UK government spending goes on health, pensions, social security, education and local government. That this is unaffordable, is confirmed by the fact that the UK now has a UK Taxpayers' Liability of over 300 per cent and a Public Sector Net Debt at 60 per cent of GDP. Both figures are projected to rise steeply.[11] The option of more increases in tax – especially on the middle classes – has already been used up. The only option now is to cut public spending, and this is now underway in the United Kingdom and Ireland, even Greece.

Spending more and more government money was not the solution it had been portrayed. Too much spending leads to chronic debt, and this in turn undermines economic growth and investment, and the confidence in government bonds. This is the true meaning of a 'Fiscal Crisis of the State'. As Adam Smith said of governments:

> They are themselves always, and without any exception, the greatest spendthrifts in the society. Let them look well after their own expense, and they may safely trust private people with theirs. If their own extravagance does not ruin the state, that of their subjects never will.

At this point in the debate, someone will usually raise the question of the 'Scandinavian Model' of high taxes and extensive government provided social services. There are some signs that this model is beginning to creak a little as the population ages.[12] Of the Scandinavian countries, only Norway seems wealthy enough (from oil revenues) to continue funding its welfare state at the levels currently available. Finland also now has a large government debt as a consequence

---

11 The PSND is projected to reach almost 70 per cent by 2011–2012.

12 Norberg, J., *In Defense of Global Capitalism* (Washington, DC: Cato Institute, 2003).

of lavish and inefficient state-run systems of education and health.[13] Sweden has been a social democracy almost unrelenting for over 100 years now. Personally, I find it a dour and cheerless place where government intervenes in all aspects of life and where 'sin taxes' are imposed with relish. Everyday items in Sweden are staggeringly expensive. For a good night out in Malmo, it is best to catch the ferry to Copenhagen. Sweden is now having to confront the possibility that its welfare state is unaffordable. Denmark is a much better place in my view, convivial, free, sophisticated and cheery. It has seen itself as a free-market, property-owning democracy[14] for 200 years now. It is also a constitutional monarchy. Its economy is based on high value export goods produced by private firms. Of the two countries, I would much rather live in Denmark where the concept of *hygge* – cosy and snug – is a way of life.

Or take the example of California. Long the most prosperous state in the United States, its share of national wealth has been decreasing steadily since 1980. This is not primarily due to other cities and states improving their performance, although this has occurred, but because, despite Silicon Valley, Google and Apple, California has been declining economically.[15] Since 2007, California has shed some 700,000 jobs, almost all of them in the private sector. Even Silicon Valley has 130,000 fewer jobs than it did in 2000. As in the UK, public spending has been rising. Between 2003 and 2007, California state and local government spending grew 31 per cent, although the state's population grew just 5 per cent. The overall tax burden as a percentage of state income has risen to the sixth-highest in the United States. According to Joel Kotkin, the reason for this is that California's radical progressive politics have moved away from an approach based on economic development and infrastructure investment, to one where 'public-sector workers, liberal lobbying organizations, and minorities ... demand ... more and more social spending'. Instead of economic development and infrastructure programmes, California spends its tax dollars on staff salaries and welfare payments. California now has a $500 billion shortfall for public sector pensions alone.

As the economy stagnates and goes into decline, the people who are squeezed are small business owners and middle-income employees of private sector firms. People vote with their feet. Between 2004 and 2007, 500,000 more Americans left California than arrived; in 2008, the net outflow reached 135,000. California now has a lower percentage of people who moved there within the last year than any state except Michigan. This further weakens the tax base and skews the state's

---

13   The Finnish welfare state is close to fiscal collapse. In 1994, the Finnish national debt was 51.7 billion euros, and by 2007, €56.1 billion. At the end of 2009, the debt was €64.3 billion. Government spending rose from €33 billion in 2000 to €46.9 billion in 2009. It is estimated that the national debt will hit €85 billion at the end of fiscal year 2010.

14   The highest rate of income tax in Denmark is 63 per cent, but this is offset by generous tax allowances, including for mortgage interest.

15   Kotkin, J., 'The Golden State's War on Itself', *The City Journal*, 20(3), Summer 2010.

demography further towards public sector employees and welfare recipients. Kotkin warns that California is becoming a 'planetary laughing-stock'. The way to recover from this, argues Kotkin, is for California to 'recognize the importance of the economic base—particularly such linchpins as agriculture, manufacturing, and trade—in re-energizing the state's economy'. In short, economic development and wealth creation.

All that this really tells is that the costs of social democracy are high and may be unaffordable into the future in the absence of a great wave of wealth creation. The question is not whether governments should regulate, but how much, and to avoid intervening when it is simply unnecessary or counter-productive. The danger is of too much government spending on welfare and vote-winning inducements, but this is in the end self-defeating, as bills have to be paid at some point. Beyond this, there is the problem of judging what is necessary intervention and how far central planning should extend into market economies. The attendant problem of governments seeking to run economies is that they frequently back the wrong horse (for example Minitel in France or various 'green' cars in Spain and Australia), employ too many people and contribute to lost dynamism and low growth.

Those who simplistically argue that the old 'free market versus government debate is over', may wish to consider the examples of New Labour and California. Market economies remain the best (perhaps only) option for economic development, with varying degrees of intervention being required. There will occasionally need to be checks on excessive behaviour and, of course, criminality by bankers and corporations, but also politicians and governments. Governments will need to assume responsibility for a welfare safety net – although how these are delivered at the point of use can take a variety of forms including, like employment training in Australia, by private companies.[16] This is especially true of health care, education and pensions. But this is not the same thing as socialism or state socialism which, as Bastiat[17] reminds us 'confuses the distinction between government and society'. The greatest danger to wealth creation will be excessive government deficits and debt, and inefficient and swollen bureaucracies.

Should parts of capitalist economies be regulated? The answer, of course is yes. In *The Wealth of Nations*, Adam Smith is quite clear on this, arguing against a free hand for banks and cartels:

> Those exertions of the natural liberty of a few individuals, which might endanger the security of the whole of society, are, and ought to be, restrained by the laws of all governments.

---

16   Carroll, J., 'Economic Consensus Calls for a Bit of Give and Take', *The Australian*, 24–25 April 2010.

17   Bastiat, E., *The Law*, 1850 [translated by Dean Russell (New York: The Foundation for Economic Education, 1998)].

In a free-market economy, government's role is to maintain stability through intelligent regulation, invest in necessary infrastructure, promote research and development and skills, but otherwise keep out of the way. Freedom requires some limitation, but not to the extent of infringing commerce unduly or restricting competition, for it is competition that is the best antidote to price-fixing and monopolies. Banks, meanwhile, should refrain from lending money for foolish schemes, like sub-prime mortgages for example. This then is a case of governments regulating but not supplanting market economies. That is to say, capitalism and democracy.

The Golden Rules of Economic Development

If the arguments put forward in this book are correct, that capitalism grows in fits and starts and booms and busts, then it will survive the 'crises' of 2008 and 2009. Capitalism and free trade will remain a dynamic system for producing, distributing and consuming goods and services in widening patterns of trade. Real economic life and wealth creation is in any event natural and part of the human condition, underscoring the ways in which societies and sociability develop. Capitalism is not a monolithic ideology, but simply the human condition in economic form. It generates the wealth for public services and government funding.

This is not a question of 'the rich getting richer and the poor getting poorer', but simply the outcome of a system which values risk and investment, and in which there are specialisms, differing skill levels and a division of labour. Everyone gets wealthier as a consequence, certainly in material goods, although the entrepreneurs, the already rich and the new rich will continue to accumulate more wealth than the average person. The 'poor' will have greater opportunities than ever before to increase their own wealth and that of their families.

As for economic theory and policy, a return to Smith's elegant, classical economics – bolstered by new knowledge of behaviour and choice – should be beneficial; seeing economic development as having similar characteristics to an ecosystem should likewise prove fruitful; understanding that growth concentrates in dynamic city regions is essential; and tempering the urge to over-engineer economies, either by monetary policy or Keynesian demand management, would seem overdue.

Taking all this into account, I am tempted to offer a few 'golden rules of wealth creation' for economists and politicians, and especially those who remain hostile to the profit motive and capitalism itself.

Rules for All of Us

1. The private sector creates wealth, not governments. In the absence of wealth-creating trading sectors of the economy, economies will slow

and stagnate, and soon decline. This means that a proportion of national economies must be made up of exports and inter-trading between cities and regions. Growth depends on trade.

2. Business owners and people setting up in business know best what is good for their business, livelihood and the place and sector of which they are part, not economists.
3. Successful economies are open-ended rather than goal-oriented; setting targets is largely a waste of time.
4. Economic growth and wealth creation depend on a process of continual innovation and improvisation.
5. Successful dynamic economies alter and change by a process of 'aesthetic drift', moving in response to myriad influences, signals and technologies.
6. Economies do not respond well to central planning; and so economic life cannot be planned; it can only be helped – or hindered.
7. Small businesses are key sites of innovation; they also happen to employ more people overall than large businesses.
8. Dynamic economies are based in real places, that is to say growing cities and regions; they are not just an aggregate of GDP across a nation.

Rules for Governments

Governments might usefully re-learn a few fundamental lessons:

1. Central planning of economies is impossible, for the simple reason that economies are open systems and are in any event likely to shift in order to circumvent 'human deductive rational intervention' by governments. People move overseas, they change their customs and routines, switch investment strategies and cancel or move projects off-shore. Therefore, governments who believe in 'firm, clear decision-making' and 'resolute purpose' in matters economic will likely fail because of the 'law of unintended consequences'.
2. Taxes on 'the wealthy', that is investors, innovators and business owners, should be reduced if possible and certainly not increased – taxes that are set too high are self-defeating. The rich people who have money to invest in new industries and businesses will simply move away if they consider taxes to be too high. This is what happened in the UK in the 1970s when the top rate of income tax was raised to 83 per cent; it happened again in New York in more recent times, and it is happening in California today.
3. Governments should not fix prices or undermine competition in any way.
4. Tariffs should not as a rule be imposed on imports, only in circumstances where an industry needs time to grow and stabilise (if at all).

5. Governments should not impose nationwide minimum wages, but leave this to the market.[18] If a minimum wage is to be set, then this should vary region-to-region depending on the labour market and living costs.

6. All things being equal, governments should spend as little money as possible, or at least keep spending on welfare programmes within a sensible limit of GDP and taxes raised. I would put this at under 40 per cent.

7. Money should under no circumstances be printed above and beyond the levels required by prudent money supply, otherwise currencies will simply fall in value. Printing money does not create value, it destroys it. Sadly, this is now occurring in the United States (for the second time) under the euphemism 'quantitative easing'.

8. Governments cannot spend their way out of a recession in the absence of an underlying economic strength and healthy, if temporarily dormant, patterns of trade. Australia survived the 2008–2009 downturn better than most, not because of large programmes of government spending (which most other countries also embarked upon), but because its economy was in good health, as were government finances. The only way to grow an economy is through private investment and innovation. Investment in productive infrastructure is also a valid concern of the state, but only if viable over the medium term.

9. The attempts to control economies by putting interest rates up and down is largely futile and counter-productive. Interest rates that are too low encourage lending, credit and spending, and a boom that is too sudden; any subsequent attempt at correction by putting rates up leads to a fall in spending and an economic downturn that is also an 'over-correction'. Interest rates should be left to markets and banks.

10. Macroeconomic policy should confine itself to maintaining stability by avoiding sudden changes in taxation, interest rates and government spending, and by understanding the business cycle.

11. Microeconomic policy should concentrate on entrepreneurial skills, firm formation, export assistance, targeted growth sectors, reducing the costs of employment and compliance, developing growth clusters and creative milieux, and promoting innovation. The aim should be to provide a more advantageous business environment and to offer incentives to innovate.

12. Trade does in fact bring peoples and countries, cities and regions together in mutual cooperation; it also helps reconcile differences and in general has a civilising influence – except in the case of fundamentalists.

Capitalism may not be perfect, but it is dynamic and it is based on markets and exchange and therefore human nature – the instinct to trade, barter, improve oneself,

---

18   In Australia, the Federal government and trades unions set 'award' or pay levels and conditions for most, if not all, sectors of the economy. This is cumbersome and bureaucratic and also skews regional pay differentials.

one's family and one's society. Markets and the everyday forms of sociability they help underpin are, moreover, the best antidote to the state over-reaching itself into the realm of individual freedoms and liberty. To repeat, the coming years will see remarkable wealth creation. The early part of the twenty-first century will be remembered as a golden age in technology, wealth creation and the arts. Millions of people will be lifted out of poverty around the world. The new upwave will be the greatest yet episode of wealth creation in human history.

Postscript

In October 2010, I was able to visit Scotland, the north of England, London and Singapore and, for some of the time, see the effects of the recession. In Singapore there was not much sign of it at all, although growth is projected, as noted earlier, to fall from around 13–15 per cent in 2009/2010 to only 6 per cent in 2010/2011, this being due in the main to falling global demand for locally-produced computers.

Scotland seemed about the same as always, pleasant but not especially dynamic outside of Glasgow and Edinburgh, although the press was full of dire warnings over the loss of 30,000 public sector jobs as a result of government spending cuts. This has become a familiar refrain in the UK, as spending cuts are rolled out, yet estimates of job losses have been reduced from just under 600,000 to just over 300,000, or about 1 per cent of all jobs. Many of these job losses will be due to 'natural wastage' and freezes on recruitment. Some former Labour Government ministers are warning that such cuts will stall the economic recovery, seemingly unable to distinguish wealth-creating activity from government spending and inefficiencies.

Yet it is true, as Peter Hall points out,[19] that many towns and cities in the north of England and Wales are now seriously dependent on public sector jobs: 39 per cent in Liverpool, 38 per cent in Newcastle, 43 per cent in Middlesbrough. In some parts of Britain, the State's share of the economy is as high as in the old Communist States of Eastern Europe: Wales at 77 per cent; Northern Ireland at 81 per cent. A cut of about 5 per cent in such places will be serious, but many of those paid off will simply retire. Some will find other jobs, some might move to find new employment. The real question, perhaps, is why it was ever thought sustainable to have so much dependency on public sector jobs. Perhaps these parts of the UK should look towards former socialist and Communist countries such as the Czech Republic, Estonia and India to see how the private sector economy grows. In any event, the projections are that the private sector will create over a million new jobs over the next four years, during the time the cuts[20] are being phased in. The cuts are

---

19   Hall, P., 'Like Living Through a Revolution', *Town and Country Planning*, 79(9), September 2010.

20   Part of the cuts are in fact reductions on projected government spending as of May 2008, and not real cuts in actual spending at all.

deemed to be necessary to restore investor confidence in the UK – more precisely, government bonds. Otherwise a fate similar to Ireland or Greece may be in store. It seems likely, as I write this, that economic growth in the UK will recover strongly in 2011 and beyond, and sterling will rise in value to reflect this.

Meanwhile, London goes on its way, creating new work, new enterprises and new jobs and spinning off economic activity into the rest of the southeast. As an economic dynamo, London has for at least 500 years been a self-generating city regional economy. It is already doing so again.

Ireland is a different matter. Here we have a country that devised a low-tax path to prosperity, but has been caught badly by the sub-prime panic, the collapse of its banks and an inability to use monetary policy to check over-lending because of its membership of the Euro. Much of the Euro's current difficulties are due to the European Central Bank having kept area-wide interest rates low to support growth in Germany. In Ireland one consequence was a property bubble as developers and individuals took out loans to build houses and shopping centres. But the main problem was that the Irish banks had been left high and dry by the sub-prime panic, and were found to have large amounts of toxic debt. Much of Ireland's public debt is due to the bailout of the banks. The option of opting out of the Euro may seem tempting, but it is too late. This would cause a flight of capital as people sell Euros ahead of the devaluation of any new currency.

The real, private sector economy in Ireland, despite the gloom, is still growing well with industrial output up 12 per cent in the past year and Irish exports per capita nearly matching those of Germany. Ireland will recover once confidence returns. The country will resume its inward-investment success story, bolstered by low corporate tax rate and its strong connections to the United States. But this will take time.

Which raises the $14 trillion question. The truth is that, despite strong growth in the economies of Asia, plus India, Russia and Brazil, a worldwide economic recovery very much hinges on prosperity in the United States and a return of consumer confidence and spending. Sadly, this still seems a distant prospect as growth in the United States struggles to reach 1 per cent for 2010. To be fair, the problems faced by the US economy have seemed daunting, although at one point in early 2008 the recovery was underway, up until, that is, the collapse of Lehman Brothers and the ensuing panic. Unemployment remains close to 10 per cent, very few new jobs are being created outside of government, the housing market is still very difficult, government debt has reached staggering levels and consumer confidence is low. But this has been compounded by the failure of the Obama administration's economic policies. The almost $1 trillion stimulus package has had little discernible effect in stoking growth, and the threat to remove tax advantages – and indeed introduce new taxes – is undermining the confidence required to encourage private sector investment and job creation. Meanwhile, the policy of 'quantitative easing' is storing up future inflation. This experiment in Neo-Keynesian economics is failing and, like the New Deal before it, will continue to fail unless and until the private sector starts to invest again. For it to do so, the

US government will need to cut rather than raise taxes, reduce rather than increase government intervention in the economy, and return nationalised industries to the market. That is to say, the Obama administration will need to end its fixation with ideology and get down to the serious business of promoting economic growth and prosperity.

If the US economy recovers in 2011, as it should, then the recession of 2008–2009 will become a painful memory. Whether the Euro survives is another question, and will depend on Germany's willingness to bail out high-debt countries such as Portugal, Spain and Italy. One suspects the tensions will become too great and the Euro will collapse. However, there are many examples from history of governments and empires over-ruling economic development for the sake of political power and control. If the history of economic development teaches us anything it is that politics should keep out of economics as far as possible.

Bibliography

Alford, R. 'What are the Origins of Fannie Mae and Freddie Mac', History News Network, 2003.

Andersen, T. M. *The Danish Economy: An International Perspective* (Copenhagen: DJOF Publishing, 2001).

Andersson, A. 'Creativity and Regional Development', *Papers of the Regional Science Association*, 56, 1985.

Armstrong, J. *In Search of Civilization: Remaking a Tarnished Idea* (London: Allen Lane, 2009).

Arnold, M. *Culture and Anarchy: An Essay in Political and Social Criticism* (Cambridge: Cambridge University Press, 1869).

Bacon, R. and Eltis, W. *Britain's Economic Problem: Too Few Producers* (London: Macmillan, 1976).

Beckman, R. *The Downwave* (London: Pan Books, 1983).

Beinhocker, E. *The Origin of Wealth* (London: Random House, 2007).

Benson, M. 'The Sensual World of Ukiyo-e Art', *The Australian Financial Review*, 9–11 May 2008.

Berry, B. J. L. *Long-Wave Rhythms in Economic Development and Political Behavior* (Baltimore: Johns Hopkins University Press, 1991).

Birth of the Chicago Union Stock Yards, The (Chicago: Chicago Historical Society, 2001).

Blanchard, O. *The State of Macro* (Cambridge, MA, MIT Working Paper, 2008).

Bolton, R. *A Brief History of Painting* (London: Robinson, 2004).

Bourdieu, P. *Taste: A Social Critique of the Judgment of Distinction* (Cambridge, MA: MIT Press, 1984).

Bowe, C. 'The Light Myth', *Adelaide Review*, July 2004.

Braudel, F. *The Perspective of the World.* Vol III of Civilization and Capitalism (London: Harper & Row, 1984).

Briggs, A. *Victorian Cities*, (London: Odhams Press, 1963).

Bronowski, J. *The Ascent of Man* (London: Book Club Associates, 1973).

Brooks, C. B. *Disaster at Lisbon: The Great Earthquake of 1755* (Long Beach, CA: Shangton Longley Press, 1994).

Brucker, G. *Renaissance Florence* (Berkeley: University of California Press, 1983).

Brugman, J. *Welcome to the Urban Revolution: How Cities Are Changing the World* (New York: Bloomsbury Press, 2009).

Brusco, S. 'The Emilian Model: Productive Decentralisation and Social Integration', *Cambridge Journal of Economics*, 6, 1982, 167–184.

Bryson, A. *From Courtesy to Civility: Changing Codes of Conduct in Early Modern England* (Oxford: Clarendon Press, 1998).

Burton, R. *Prague: A Cultural and Literary History* (Oxford: Signal Books, 2003).

Calomiris, C. W. and Schweikar, L. 'The Panic of 1857: Origins, Transmission and Containment', *Journal of Economic History*, 51(4), December 1991.

Campagni, R. 'The Concept of Innovative Milieu and its Relevance for Public Policy in Europe's Lagging Regions', *Papers in Regional Science*, 74(4), 1995, 317–340.

Chang, J. and Halliday, J. *Mao: The Unknown Story* (London: Jonathan Cape, 2005).

Cole, H. L. and Ohanian, L. E. 'New Deal Prolonged the Great Depression', *The Australian*, 5 February 2009.

Colin Campbell, Lady, *Guide to Being a Modern Lady* (London: Heterodox, 1986).

Carroll, J. *The Wreck of Western Culture* (Melbourne: Scribe, 2004).

Carroll, J. 'Economic Consensus Calls for a Bit of Give and Take', *The Australian*, 24–25 April 2010.

Cashin, P. and Sahay, R. 'Regional Economic Growth and Convergence in India', *Finance and Development*, March, 1996, 49–52.

Chester, D. K. 'The 1755 Lisbon Earthquake', *Progress in Physical Geography*, 25(3), 2001, 363–383.

Clark, J., Freeman, C. and Soete, L. 'Long Waves, Inventions, and Innovations', *Futures*, 15, 1981.

Cronon, W. *Nature's Metropolis: Chicago and the Great West* (New York: W. W. Norton, 1992 [1991]).

Diggle, P. and Ormerod, P. *Be Bold for Growth* (London: Centre for Policy Studies, March 2010).

Dong, S. *Shanghai: The Rise and Fall of a Decadent City* (New York: HarperCollins, 2000).

Driver, P. *Manchester Pieces* (London: Picador, 1996).

Evans, D. M. *The History of the Commercial Crisis 1857–1858* (Newton Abbot: David and Charles, 1859).

'Fannie Mae Eases Credit to Aid Mortgage Lending', *New York Times*, 30 September 1999.

Ferguson, N. *Empire: How Britain Made the Modern World* (London: Penguin, 2004).

Ferguson, N. *The Ascent of Money: A Financial History of the World* (New York: Allen Lane, 2008).

Field, C. and Field, P. *Scandinavian Design* (Copenhagen: Taschen, 2002).

Fisher, I. *100% Money* (New York: Adelphi Company, 1934).

Foster, J. *Productivity, Creative Destruction and Innovation Policy* (Sydney: The Australian Business Foundation, February 2010).

Freeman, C. and Soete, L. *The Economics of Industrial Innovation* (Cambridge, MA: MIT Press, 1997).

Freeman, C., Clark, J. and Soete, L. *Unemployment and Technical Innovation: A Study of Long Waves and Economic Development* (New York Greenwood Press, 1982).

Friedman, M. *Capitalism and Freedom* (Chicago: University of Chicago Press, 1962).

Gardner, H. *Art, Mind and Brain: A Cognitive Approach to Creativity* (New York: Basic Books, 1982).

Garreau, J. *Edge City: Life on the New Frontier* (New York: Anchor/Doubleday, 1991).

Geddes, P. *Cities in Evolution* (London: Williams & Norgate, 1915).

Gerkens, K. *Strategies and Tools for Shrinking Cities – the Example of Leipzig*, paper presented to the International Cities, Town Centres and Communities Conference, June 2005, Capricorn Coast, Queensland.

Giddens, A. *The Third Way. The Renewal of Social Democracy* (Cambridge: Polity, 1998).

Girouard, M. *Cities and People* (New Haven: Yale University Press, 1985).

Glaser, E. 'Are Cities Dying?', *Journal of Economic Perspectives*, 12, 1998, 139–160.

Hall P. *Cities in Civilisation* (London: Weidenfeld and Nicolson, 1998).

Hall, P. *Cities of Tomorrow* (Oxford: Blackwell, 1998).

Hall, P. 'Like Living Through a Revolution', *Town and Country Planning*, 79(9), September 2010.

Hall, P. and Preston, P. *The Carrier Wave: New Information Technology and the Geography of Innovation* (London: Unwin Hyman, 1988).

Handy, C. *The Age of Unreason* (London: Century Business, 1990).

Hansen, A. L. and Andersen, H. T. 'Creative Copenhagen: Globalisation, Urban Governance and Social Change', *European Planning Studies*, 9(7), 2001.

Havel, V. *Redevelopment* (London: Faber & Faber, 1990).

Hayek von, F. A. *The Road to Serfdom* (London: George Routledge and Sons, 1944).

Herman, A. *The Scottish Enlightenment* (London: Fourth Estate, 2003).

HM Treasury. *Trend Growth: New Evidence and Prospects* (London: HMSO, December 2006).

Hollingsworth, A. *Modern Design* (Gibbs Smith, 2008).

Horne, D. *The Lucky Country* (Harmondsworth: Penguin Books, 1964).

Howkins, J. *The Creative Economy: How People Make Money from Ideas* (New York: Penguin, 2001).

Howley, K. M. 'Rate Rise Pushes Housing, Economy to "Blood Bath"', Bloomberg, 20 June 2007.

Hughes, J. R. T. *The Commercial Crisis of 1857* (Oxford: Oxford University Press, 1956).

Hutchings, A. 'Consistent Vision: The Planning of Metropolitan Adelaide', in Freestone, R. (ed.), *Spirited Cities* (Sydney: The Federation Press, 1983).

Hutton, W. *Them and Us: Politics, Greed and Inequality* (London: Little Brown, 2010).

Ishiguro, K. *An Artist of the Floating World* (London: Faber & Faber, 1986).

Jacobs, J. *The Economy of Cities* (London: Jonathan Cape, 1969).

Jacobs, J. *Cities and the Wealth of Nations* (New York: Random House, 1984).

Jacobs, J. *The Nature of Economies* (New York: Vintage, 2000).

Jones, E. *Metropolis: The World's Great Cities* (Oxford: Oxford University Press, 1990).

Kames, Lord. *Historical Law Tracts* (Edinburgh, 1759).

Kanagawa Prefectural Government. *The History of Kanagawa* (Yokohama, 1985).

Kellner, P. *The Crisis of Social Democracy* (London: Demos, September 2010).

Kendrick, T. D. *The Lisbon Earthquake* (London: Methuen, 1956).

Kennedy, M. *Portrait of Manchester* (Manchester: Robert Hale, 1970).

Keynes, J. M. *The General Theory of Employment, Interest and Money* (London: Macmillan, 1936).

Keynes, J. M. *A Treatise on Money: The Pure Theory of Money* (London: Macmillan, 1971).

Kierkegaard, S. *Either/Or* (London: Penguin, 1992).

Kirman, A. 'The Future of Economic Theory', in Kirman, A. and Gerard-Varet, L.-A., *Economics Beyond the Millennium* (Oxford: Oxford University Press, 1999).

Klaus, V. *Renaissance: The Rebirth of Liberty at the Heart of Europe* (New York: Cato Institute, 1997).

Kleinknecht, A. *Innovation Patterns in Crisis and Prosperity: Schumpeter's Long Cycle Reconsidered* (London: Macmillan, 1987).

Kondratieff, N. D. *The Long Wave Cycle* (New York: Richardson and Snyder, 1984).

Kostof, S. *The City Assembled* (London: Thames and Hudson, 1992).

Kotkin, J. 'The Golden State's War on Itself', *The City Journal*, 20(3), Summer 2010.

Kuhn, T. S. *The Structure of Scientific Revolutions* (Chicago: University of Chicago Press, 1962).

Kunstler, J. *The Geography of Nowhere: The Rise and Decline of America's Man-Made Landscape* (New York: Touchstone, 1994).

Kuznets, S. 'Schumpeter's Business Cycles', *American Economic Review*, 30, 1940, 250–271.

Lambourne, L. *Japonisme: Cultural Crossings Between Japan and the West* (London: Phaidon Press, 2005).

Lancaster, J. *Whoops! Why Everyone Owes Everyone and No One Can Pay* (New York: Allen Lane, 2010).

Landsburg, S. *The Armchair Economist* (New York: The Free Press, 1993).

Lane, R. *Hokusai: Life and Work* (New York: E. P. Dutton, 1989).

Langmead, D. and Johnson, D. L. *City of Adelaide Plan: Fiction and Fact* (Adelaide: Wakefield Press, 1986).

Leavis, F. R. *Mass Civilisation and Minority Culture* (Cambridge: Cambridge University Press, 1930).

Leinberger, C. B. *The Option of Urbanism: Investing in a New American Dream* (Washington, DC: Island Press, 2008).

Lopez, R. S. 'The Trade of Medieval Europe', in Postan M. and Rich E. E. (eds), *The Cambridge Economic History of Europe, 2: Trade and Industry in the Middle Ages*, pp 257–354 (Cambridge: Cambridge University Press, 1952).

Lowenstein, R. *The End of Wall Street* (Melbourne: Scribe, 2010).

Lynch, M. *The Early Modern Town in Scotland* (North Ryde: Croom Helm, 1987).

Mager, N. H. *The Kondratieff Waves* (New York: Praeger, 1987).

Manetti, A. *The Life of Brunelleschi*, edited by Howard Saalman and translated by Catherine Enggass (Philadelphia: Pennsylvania State University Press, 1970).

Manne, R. and McKnight, D. *Goodbye to All That? On the Failure of Neo-Liberalism and the Urgency of Change* (Sydney: Black Inc, 2010).

Marshall, A. *Principles of Economics* (London: Macmillan, 1920).

Marx, K. *Capital: A Critique of Political Economy: Volume 3, Part 1, The Process of Capitalist Production as a Whole, 1867* (New York: Cosimo Books, 1996).

Matthews, R. C. O. 'Why has Britain had Full Employment since the War?' *The Economic Journal*, 1968.

Maxwell, K. *Pombal: Paradox of the Enlightenment* (Cambridge: Cambridge University Press, 1995).

Mensch, G. *Stalemate in Technology: Innovations Overcome the Depression* (Cambridge, MA: Ballinger, 1979).

Miller, D. L. *City of the Century: The Epic of Chicago and the Making of America* (New York: Simon and Schuster, 1996).

Modelski, G. and Thompson, W. R. *Globalization as an Evolutionary Process* (London: Taylor and Francis, 1996).

Montgomery, J. *The New Wealth of Cities: City Dynamics and the Fifth Wave* (Aldershot: Ashgate, 2007).

Montgomery, J. 'Urban Sociability', *Town & Country Planning*, 76(10), October 2007.

Montgomery, J. 'Manners Maketh the City', *Journal of Urban Design*, 13(2), June 2008, 159–162.

Montgomery, J. 'Social Engineers Make Bad Bankers', *The Australian*, 1 October 2008.

Mumford, L. *The Culture of Cities* (New York: Harcourt, Brace, 1938).

Mumford, L. *The City in History* (New York: Harvest, 1961).

Murray, F. 'Flexible Specialisation in the "Third Italy"', *Capital & Class*, 11(3), Winter 1987, 84–95.

Musil, R. *The Man Without Qualities* (London: Picador, 1997).

Newman, P. and Smith, I. 'Cultural Production, Place and Politics on the South Bank of the Thames', *International Journal of Urban and Regional Research*, 24(1), 2000, 9–24.

Norberg, J. *In Defence of Global Capitalism* (Washington, DC: Cato Institute, 2003).

Ockman, J. *Out of Ground Zero: Case Studies in Urban Reinvention* (New York: Prestel, 2002).

O'Rourke, P. J. *On The New Wealth of Nations* (London: Allen & Unwin, 2007).

Pacyga, D. A. *Chicago: A Biography* (Chicago: University of Chicago Press, 2009).

Parto, S. 'Innovation and Economic Activity: An Institutional Analysis of the Role of Clusters in Industrializing Economies', *Journal of Economic Issues*, 42, 2008.

Pasqui, G. 'The Perspective of the Infinite City', *Planning, Theory and Practice*, 5(3), September 2004, 381–389.

Pearce, N. 'Measured Progress', *RSA Journal*, Summer 2010, 15–19.

Perez, C. *Technological Revolutions and Financial Capital: The Dynamics of Bubbles and Golden Ages* (Cheltenham: Edward Elgar, 2002).

Phillipson, N. *Adam Smith: An Enlightened Life* (London: Allen Lane, 2010).

Pirenne, H. 'Les Periodes de l'Histoire sociale du Capitalisme', *Bulletin de l'Academie Royale Belgique*, 5, 1914, 258–299.

Pirenne, H. *Medieval Cities: Their Origins and the Revival of Trade*, translated by F. D. Halsey (Princeton: Princeton University Press, 1969).

Porter, M. *The Competitive Advantage of Nations* (London: Collier Macmillan, 1990).

Postan, C. *The Cambridge Economic History of Europe: Trade and Industry in the Middle Ages, Volume 2* (Cambridge: Cambridge University Press, 1987).

Priem, R. *Dutch Masters* (Melbourne: National Gallery of Victoria, 2005).

Raban, J. *Soft City* (London: Hamish Hamilton, 1974).

'Reserve Bank Blundered: Costello', *The Australian*, 29 October 2008.

Rising Above the Gathering Storm: Energising and Employing America for a Brighter Economic Future (Washington, DC: National Academies Press, 2008).

Roover de, R. *The Rise and Decline of the Medici Bank* (Cambridge, MA: Harvard University Press, 1963).

Rostow, W. W. *The Stages of Economic Growth* (Cambridge: Cambridge University Press, 1990).

Rudd, K. 'The Global Financial Crisis', *The Monthly*, February 2009.

Sainsbury Report. *The Race to the Top: A Review of Government's Science and Innovation Policies* (London: HMSO, 2007).

Sabel, C. *Work and Politics* (Cambridge: Cambridge University Press, 1982).

Salmon, T. J. *Borrowstounness and district, being historical sketches of Kinneil, Carriden, and Bo'ness, c. 1550–1850* (Edinburgh: Scot W. Hodge, 1913).

Schama, S., *The Embarrassment of Riches: An Interpretation of Dutch Culture in the Golden Age* (Berkeley: University of California Press, 1987).

Schumpeter, J. *Business Cycles* (New York: McGraw-Hill, 1939; Philadelphia: Porcupine Press, reprinted 1982).

Schumpeter, J. *Capitalism, Socialism and Democracy* (London: George Allen and Unwin, 1976; originally published 1943).

Sennet, R. *The Conscience of the Eye: The Design and Social Life of Cities* (London: Faber & Faber, 1990).

Sforzi, F. 'The Geography of Industrial Districts in Italy', in Goodman, E. and Bamford, J. (eds), *Small Firms and Industrial Districts in Italy* (London: Routledge, 1989).

Singer, P. *Pushing Time Away: My Grandfather and the Tragedy of Jewish Vienna* (Sydney: HarperCollins, 2003).

Smith, A. *The Wealth of Nations* (London: Penguin Classics, 1986; originally published 1776).

Smith, A. *Theory of Moral Sentiments* (London: Prometheus, 2000).

Smith, C. S., *The Plan of Chicago: Daniel Burnham and the Remaking of the American City* (Chicago: University of Chicago Press, 2006).

Smith, R., Lawson, A. and Hume, J. R., *The Making of Scotland: A Comprehensive Guide to the Growth of its Cities, Towns, and Villages* (Edinburgh: Canongate, 2002).

Snow, C. P. *The Two Cultures* (Cambridge: Cambridge University Press, 1964).

Stiglitz, J. *Freefall: Free Markets and the Sinking of the Global Economy* (New York: Allen Lane, 2010).

Swenson, John W. *Jean Baptiste Point du Sable – The Founder of Modern Chicago* (Chicago: Early Chicago Inc, 1999).

Taine, H. *Notes on England*, translated by E. Hyams (London: Thames and Hudson, 1957).

Törnqvist, G. 'Creativity and the Renewal of Regional Life', in Buttimer, A. (ed.), *Creativity and Context* (Lund: Gleerup, 1983).

Truss, L. *Talk to the Hand: The Utter Bloody Rudeness of Everyday Life* (London: Profile Books, 2005).

Unglow, J. *The Lunar Men: The Friends Who made the Future* (London: Faber & Faber, 2002).

Webb, F. *A History of Hong Kong* (London: HarperCollins, 1993).

Wilson, Mark R., 'Union Stock Yard and Transit Co.', in Grossman, J. R., Durkin Keating, A. and Ruff, J. L. (eds), *The Encyclopedia of Chicago* (Chicago: University of Chicago Press, 2004).

Index

Bold page numbers indicate figures, *italic* numbers indicate tables.